THE ISLAND COOKBOOK

TRADITIONAL RECIPES FROM THE ISLE OF WIGHT

THE ISLAND COOKBOOK

TRADITIONAL RECIPES FROM THE ISLE OF WIGHT

JOHANNA JONES

ISLAND BOOKS
NEWPORT, ISLE OF WIGHT

First Edition 1984
Published in Island Books 1993

Recipes from *Pot Luck* © May Byron. Reprinted by permission of Hodder and Stoughton Ltd. Recipes from *The Isle of Wight Cookery Book* reprinted by permission of the Isle of Wight County Federation of Women's Institutes.

Pencil drawings by Frank Basford. Line drawings by Louise Burston and Helen Backhouse.
Photographs taken by Mike Edwards.
View of Carisbrooke Castle by permission of the Ancient Monuments Secretariat, Department of the Environment. The fireplace at Hanover House, Brook, by permission of Jane and John Nickerson.
Back cover: photograph taken by Jack Jones.

Designed by Louise Burston

Typeset by Pauline Newton

Island Books is an imprint of Ravenswood Publications Ltd, London

Distributed by Hammerton Book Services, 19 High Street, Newport, Isle of Wight PO30 1SS

Printed and bound by Yelf Printers Ltd, Newport, Isle of Wight PO30 5AU

ISBN 1 898198 00 4

ACKNOWLEDGEMENTS

I am grateful to the publishers, Hodder and Stoughton Ltd., for their permission to use the Isle of Wight recipes included by May Byron in her book *Pot Luck*, a fine collection of old county recipes first published in 1914. I am equally indebted to the Island County Federation of Women's Institutes for allowing me to include some Victorian recipes from the wide selection of recipes and household hints collected by my fellow W.I. members in 1934 and published today as *The Isle of Wight Cookery Book.*

Mrs. Margaret Oglander was more than kind in making me welcome in the several visits I made to choose recipes from the Nunwell 'Receipts' Book. I also thank Mrs. Winifred Drudge who so generously lent me her handwritten cookery book so that I could make my selection.

I would also like to thank Mrs. Ellen Dowden, whose recollections of the food she ate as a child and the cost of the ingredients at the end of the nineteenth century, were so valuable. I am grateful also to Clifford Matthews who took time to tell me his own methods of cooking fish, and Virginia Abbot who spent many hours recalling for me the recipes she enjoyed as a child growing up in Isle of Wight County, Virginia.

In addition, I thank other friends for special recipes: Eileen Jones, Miriam Harrison, Hilton Matthews, Bob Fewtrell and the Community of Sisters at St. Dominic's Priory, Carisbrooke, and also today's recipe makers who allowed me to include some of their favourites: Joyce Bale, Una Samuel, Hannah Hutchinson, Jane Nickerson and Helena Hewston. My thanks to all of them for the help they have given me. Finally, I thank my husband, Jack, for his help and encouragement.

Johanna Jones
Woodlands Cottage

CONTENTS

INTRODUCTION

In the thirty years we have lived on the Isle of Wight we have had two very different homes. Our first home was a fourteenth century tower in Carisbrooke Castle. Now we live in an early nineteenth century cottage in a hollow of the downs about a mile away but still in sight of the Castle walls. There couldn't be a greater contrast between the high Gothic rooms in the medieval tower and the snug, low-ceilinged cottage, but both share the same happy quality – they are both quiet, restful places in which to live. At the Castle, even at the busiest time of year, our living room, high above the courtyard, was a peaceful place to sit. The cottage, sheltered by a little hanging copse, is even quieter – surrounded by fields and bounded still by those sunken lanes that all who know the Island love, crimson and white with campion and lady smock in early Summer, and in Autumn, golden brown with tall fronds of bracken.

The Island has a fascinating history with Carisbrooke Castle as its centre. Living in the Castle, I found myself wanting to discover more about the everyday life of Islanders down the centuries. The Island has received a rich legacy from the past: a Royal Palace, elegant manors, comfortable farms and old cottages all with their stories to tell. It is quite easy to study the bricks and stones that are the fabric of people's homes but much more difficult to find out what went on in the kitchens and what was carried onto their dining tables. But as I researched I discovered recipes and snippets of Island history which I noted for future use. This collection was the beginning of *The Island Cookbook*.

But soon the book took over and determined for itself what recipes should be included! Interesting examples of Island cooking, past and present, came to me to make a collection that is truly an *Island* cookery book, reflecting Island life over three centuries, from all levels of society – royalty, gentlemen, and cottagers.

9

The food people eat mirrors their way of life. The recipes from the superb collection made by the ladies of the Oglander Family at Nunwell reflect the time and skill spent in cooking and preserving in a gentleman's household in the seventeenth and eighteenth centuries. The well-thumbed handwritten cookery book of an Island farmer's wife, who began married life in the 1920s, was another source of recipes from a period that already seems part of another world. The spoken recollections of a grandmother, now in her mid-nineties, recreate the meals her mother made when she was a little girl at the end of Queen Victoria's reign. And the recipe for an eggless cake, baked during the last war, will recall for many of us memories of the problems of cooking in wartime — and the good results often achieved in spite of the difficulties.

The Isle of Wight is essentially a rural community, so these are country recipes; neither elaborate in their ingredients nor expensive to make. Traditional cookery contains a wealth of puddings and here you will find some that are delicious and very easy to prepare. And you will find that many of these quick, simple recipes adapt themselves easily to modern life — the savouries that concluded a Victorian dinner make highly appetizing TV snacks.

My book is a glimpse into the kitchens of Island cooks in the past, and the present. I hope it will find a place in your kitchen to give you a taste of a delightful island, the Isle of Wight.

COTTAGE COOKERY

Bacon and Onion Roll
Bacon and Cabbage
Beef Stew
Rabbit Pie with Pork Slices
Rabbit Pie with Bacon
Economy Pea-shell Soup
Split Pea Soup
Victorian Pease Soup
Vegetable Soup
Syrup Pudding
Spotty Dick
Godshill Bread Pudding
Isle of Wight Trifle

The Island is famous for its attractive cottages. This is especially true of the central and southern parishes where good stone houses were built in the eighteenth century, as well as white chalk clunch cottages, topped with deep thatched roofs, which remain some of the prettiest homes we have today. At the end of the century brick began to be used, sometimes with stone and flint. The older cottages were usually only one large room with an exactly similar room above. Our own cottage, near Carisbrooke, began life just like that. It was built about 1800 of a mixture of materials, limestone, ironstone and flint, with brick quoins and facings for the windows and door, and was covered with a thatched roof.

Inside, at one gable end, was a huge open fireplace and at the other a ladder-like staircase led straight up into one large bedroom on the upper floor. By the greatest good fortune I met someone whose grandparents lived in our cottage at the end of the nineteenth century, which is the date of my earliest cottage recipes. They had very little furniture, but used it cleverly to make their home comfortable. There was a high-backed wooden settle placed at right angles to the wall just behind the door so that it made a kind of entrance lobby and kept away the draughts from the fire and living part of the room. Upstairs, the parents made two bedrooms by fastening long upright boards to the head of the wide bedstead so that they were separated from the open landing where the rest of the family slept.

The walls are two feet thick! Under the deep thatch it would have been warm in winter and cool in Summer. But originally it would have been very dark. The two windows were set one each side of the door facing up the sloping garden to the hanging copse on the hillside below the down. On the opposite side the cottage overlooks a lovely hidden valley, folded into the curve of a gently-rounded down that shuts us off from Carisbrooke.

It is one of our greatest pleasures to look out at that view from the window we cut into the wall of the old cottage, but the nineteenth century cottager would not have wanted windows in the cold side of the house.

There was no time for looking at views: the family's interest was in the garden, two-thirds of an acre, enough for the cottager to work in his own time without becoming too tired for his work on the farm.

Wages were low and families large. Meals had to be economical and satisfying. The recipes that follow prove just how skilful the cottage housewife was in providing tasty and economical food for her family.

Pork and bacon were the mainstay of most households who would all have a small pig-sty and run. Boiling up the mash was the housewife's daily chore. To watch the pig grow big and fat was to see a full larder growing before her eyes! My oldest cottage recipe states simply: "An Isle of Wight Dish. Boil bacon, potatoes, cabbage and suet pudding all in 1 pot". Mrs. Ellen Dowden, aged 94, tells me how her mother cooked this dish when she was a small girl in the 1890s living in Holyrood Street in Newport. She calls it "Hock of bacon and 'tatty' net vegetables". The bacon, swedes and cabbage, together with an enormous suet pudding, were boiled in the copper, each vegetable tied in a separate 'tatty' net, or fine cloth, and the pudding well wrapped in a strong cloth. Each ingredient had to be lowered into the boiling water to allow it just the right time to simmer to perfection and for the taste of the bacon to permeate the vegetables. And there they had a complete, economical meal of four dishes, cooked all together over one heat. Try this recipe from Mrs. Dowden for a good, filling main course.

BACON AND ONION ROLL

½ lb. bacon, 1 large onion, ½ lb. stiff suet pastry. * Cut the bacon and onion into small pieces. Roll out the pastry on a floured board and cover it with the bacon and onion mixture, leaving about an inch round the edge. Roll up the pastry, sealing the edges firmly with water. Put the roll in a wet, scalded cloth (the cloth was put in boiling water so that the pastry did not stick), and tie up firmly. Boil steadily for 1½–2 hours.

Preparing butcher's suet is time-consuming but makes marvellous pastry. Of course, packet suet can be used instead. In 1890, says Mrs. Dowden, a large piece of suet cost 1d (½p), the flour 1½d (1p). Suet pastry was popular with cottagers because it was cheap to make and increased in bulk during boiling.

*SUET PASTRY (old style)

½ lb. butcher's suet, 1½ lbs. self-raising flour, pinch of salt, water to mix. Remove the suet from the membrane that surrounds it and then chop or grate it finely, dredging it with flour to stop it from sticking. Mix with the rest of the flour, add the salt and mix with the water to a pliable dough.

~~~~~~~~

Another old Islander once remarked to me that he thought the Island must have been full of the smell of boiling cabbage in the old days. He had a vague memory of seeing saucepans full of cabbage simmering on kitchen hobs with somewhere about them the smell of bacon.

BACON AND CABBAGE

A bacon joint, one medium cabbage, a few medium-sized potatoes. Put the bacon in a large saucepan and cover with water. Bring to the boil and add chopped cabbage. Leave to simmer for about 1½ hours. Now add the potatoes and allow to simmer for another half-hour. Remove bacon and serve with the vegetables.

'Stew' is a word that seems to have gone out of favour, replaced by the superior 'casserole' that hints at French cooking as compared with the drab English version. But a good rich stew, prepared cottage-fashion, with steam rising from the pot and savoury smells filling the air is something to welcome you on a cold day! The Dowden family's stew comprised: 1 lb. beef cuttings — 4d (2p), with onions, carrots, swedes and dumplings to go with it. The meat could either be fried first to seal in the juices or rolled in flour and then simmered with the vegetables. The second method was probably the one used in most Victorian cottages but here is a more modern version which I use regularly.

BEEF STEW

1 lb. stewing steak, 2 onions, carrots, swedes or turnips if you like them, fat the size of a walnut to fry, 1 pint of water, bouquet garni* or any mixture of dried or fresh herbs you like, seasoning. Cut the meat into small pieces, removing all the fat. Fry the meat quickly, turning the pieces until every surface has been sealed. Put the meat aside, and fry the onions lightly in the remaining fat. Remove them. Add the scraps of meat left from trimming the steak (not the fat) to the pan, together with a pint of water and simmer this for 2 or 3 minutes. Strain off the liquid and put it and the meat into a thick-based saucepan or casserole dish. Slice the rest of the vegetables and add them to the stew. Season well and add either a bouquet garni,* or a mixture of dried or fresh herbs that you like, in a small cotton or muslin bag (you can buy these), setting it in the middle of the meat and vegetables. Bring the stew to the boil and let it simmer slowly for about three hours until the meat is tender. If you put the stew in the oven set it at low heat, 275F, Mark 1. I use my Slow Cooker, where the hot stew can be left at the right temperature to cook for 5—6 hours. I also like to thicken the stew at the end of cooking, mixing a tablespoonful of flour with the liquid and then stirring it into the stew.

*BOUQUET GARNI

Two or three sprigs of parsley, a sprig of thyme, a bayleaf.

DUMPLINGS

Dumplings were put in the stew, made from the usual suet pastry (see recipe p. 15). Shape the paste into small balls and add them to the stew about half an hour before you want to eat it.

The secret of the rich flavour of cottage stews was that they were often based on a stockpot left simmering on the hob. All stews and casseroles improve with a second cooking — try making the stew the day before you want it and then reheating it.

~~~~~~~

Those of us with country gardens will be all too aware of rabbits all around us, busy stuffing themselves with our greens! So they have for centuries ever since they escaped from the warrens where they were originally kept as a luxury food for the families of gentlefolk like the Oglanders. But they were still the monopoly of the gentry and aristocracy until the Ground Game Act of 1881 which allowed farmers to kill rabbits and hares on their land without having first to get permission from the landowner. This meant cheap rabbits in the shops and more chances for the cottagers to obtain cheap meat.

RABBIT PIE WITH SLICES OF PORK

A Victorian recipe from Mrs. Dowden. *1 rabbit, jointed, 3 slices of pork to taste, pastry made from self-raising flour and pure pig's lard (Mrs. Dowden's mother bought this as a bladder of lard from the pork butcher), seasoning.* A dish was lined with pastry, the rabbit and sliced pork were put in with seasoning, a little liquid was added (stock or water to half way up the dish), the pie was covered and cooked in a moderate oven for two hours.

RABBIT PIE WITH BACON

A more modern pie but one with the taste of a real country meal. *1 whole rabbit, jointed, or a packet of diced rabbit meat, ½ lb. streaky bacon rashers, 1 medium onion, seasoning, about ½ pint stock or water, pinch of mace, chopped parsley or chopped mixed herbs (I use a mixture of marjoram, sweet basil and thyme), a little seasoned flour.* Soak the rabbit flesh in cold water overnight, then strain. Dry the meat and roll it in seasoned flour. Remove the rind from the bacon and cut it into strips. Slice up the onion thinly. Mix together the bacon, onion, parsley or herbs, and seasoning. Put layers of rabbit and the bacon mixture into a pie dish. Add the stock or water to half fill the dish but do not let the filling come above the edge of the dish. Cover with short crust pastry.* Bake in a hot oven, 400F, Mark 6, for half an hour until the pastry is brown. Reduce the heat to 375F, Mark 5, cover the crust with cooking foil, and continue cooking for another hour.

Wild thyme.

When I was learning to cook in the years following the last war we had a marvellous teacher who always assumed her students would go to live in the farthest outposts of what was then the Empire! Consequently, she taught us to rely on relative quantities and not on given amounts in recipes. Over the years I hear her saying, "half fat to flour" for pastry. Once you know this you cannot go wrong in making simple short crust pastry.

*SHORT CRUST PASTRY

8 ozs. plain flour, 4 ozs. fat (margarine, or a mixture of margarine and lard), pinch of salt, water to mix. Rub the fat into the flour and salt until it looks like fine breadcrumbs. Add the water gradually until you have a soft paste. Cover the pastry and let it rest for about twenty minutes in a cool place. Roll out on a floured board. (Best would be a piece of marble — a real treasure for pastry making was the top of an old washstand.) Pastry should be made quickly, handled lightly, and kept as cool as possible.

~~~~~~~

ECONOMY PEA-SHELL SOUP

Boil *pea-shells* until tender with *a bone or a small quantity of finely chopped meat.* Pound the pea-shells and meat in a mortar and rub through a hair sieve. (Today, put them in a blender for a minute or two.) Add the liquor the pea-shells are boiled in, sufficient to make the soup the required thickness. Add *pepper, salt, a little sugar, cream or milk, a little onion (previously fried in butter), and a bone.* Simmer gently for a few minutes. Note: if cream is used it should be stirred in just before serving, not boiled with the soup.

~~~~~~~

18

SPLIT PEA SOUP

½ lb. split peas, 2 onions, 2 carrots, ½ a small swede, a meat bone. Put in a saucepan the bone, onions, swede and carrots. Add water to cover and simmer until the vegetables are cooked. Soak the split peas overnight in cold water. Drain them and put them into a saucepan with 2 pints of cold water. Simmer for about two hours until they are soft. Add them to the vegetables and simmer together for a few minutes. This is how Mrs. Dowden's mother made it.

A bone makes a great difference to soups. Both the above recipes include one as the cooks knew that the bone would add not only fragments of meat but a richer quality to the finished soup.

PEASE SOUP

Another Victorian recipe using ham or chicken liquor. *1 lb. split peas (or dried peas), 1 onion, liquor from a boiled ham or chicken, a little pepper.* Soak the split peas overnight and drain. Place them in a saucepan with the onion, sliced. Cover them with cold water and bring to the boil. Allow them to simmer for about two hours until the peas are tender. Drain them and put through a sieve (or electric blender). Return the pea pulp to the saucepan and add to it the liquor from a boiled ham or chicken to make the soup the required thickness. Grind in a little pepper to taste. Put on to simmer for five minutes, and it is ready. Note: be careful to taste the soup as you add the liquid. If it is too salty, make up with water.

19

VEGETABLE SOUP

1 small onion, 1 medium size carrot, 2 medium size potatoes, 2 cabbage leaves, a small piece of swede or turnip. Other vegetables can be included as you like; mushroom stalks, thinly sliced, add a good flavour. ¾ pt. cold water, 1 oz. margarine, pepper and salt to season. Slice all the vegetables thinly. Put the margarine into a saucepan and add the vegetables. Cover with greased paper or foil, fitting closely on the vegetables. Leave to sweat for fifteen minutes on the lowest heat. You should be able to put a sharp pointed knife through them at the end of that time. Add the water and seasoning (but be sparing of the pepper and salt). Bring to simmering point and let the vegetables cook for fifteen to twenty minutes. When they are ready you will be able to crush them easily with a wooden spoon. Put the mixture into a blender or mash it well with a potato masher (I think this latter method gives a more interesting texture than the smooth result of the blender, but this is a matter of taste). These ingredients make a very thick soup which can be thinned with milk or water. It freezes well.

'A View of a kitchen at Steepe Hill, Nr. Ventnor' by John Nixon reproduced by permission of the Trustees of Carisbrooke Castle Museum from a watercolour presented to the Museum collection by the Friends of the Museum.

Suet puddings were great favourites of our grandparents and great-grandparents. The Victorian cottage housewife soon worked off the extra calories, cooking food in heavy pots and pans, beating and stirring the clothes in the wash-tub with her long-handled three-legged 'dolly', or a metal 'posser', and rubbing garments on a ridged wash-board with a large bar of soap, then hauling the wet clothes out of the copper before putting them through a heavy wooden mangle. Ironing with the solid metal flat-irons was also hard work; one iron was kept heating on the hob, or in a special niche at the back of the open fireplace, while another one was in use. Here are two puddings which were special favourites.

SYRUP PUDDING

A modern version of the original substantial pudding, sufficient for 4–5 people. *3 ozs. suet, 6 ozs. self-raising flour, 2 ozs. fine breadcrumbs, 2 ozs. sugar, pinch of salt, water or milk to mix, Golden Syrup.* Grease a pudding basin well (1½–2 pt. capacity). Make the pastry with the dry ingredients, adding water or milk to make a soft dough. Roll the pastry out into a round ¼–½ inch thick, sufficient to line the basin with enough left over for a lid and several layers (the lid will take about a quarter of the pastry). Lift the remaining pastry into the basin and press firmly to fit the bottom and sides. Trim off the excess pastry and from this cut your layers. Put a generous amount of syrup next in the bottom, then a pastry layer, then more syrup, and so on until the basin is full. Damp the edges of the pastry and cover with the lid, gently pressing it into place. Cover with greaseproof paper and with foil. Steam for two hours. You must use a lot of syrup to make this pudding really well, but when it is turned out, soaked in the sweet golden juice, it is something to remember!

~~~~~~~

SPOTTY DICK

The Victorian recipe made a very substantial pudding. It was made from ½ lb. butcher's suet (a large piece cost 1d), 1½ lbs. self-raising flour (cost 1½d), whatever dried fruit was available, and sugar to taste (the Victorians liked their puddings very sweet). I have adapted the recipe to make a pudding to serve 4—5 people. *3 ozs. suet, 6 ozs. self-raising flour, 2 ozs. fine breadcrumbs, pinch of salt, 4—6 ozs. currants, 2 ozs. sugar, water (or milk) to mix.* Mix all the dry ingredients together and mix to a soft dough with water or milk. Put into a well-greased china basin (1½—2 pt. capacity). Cover with a greaseproof paper and then with cooking foil. The paper can be pleated in the middle to allow for the pudding rising, and it is tucked in round the rim of the basin. Tie the foil firmly over the basin, leaving room for expansion. Steam for two hours.

~~~~~~

Bread pudding was part of every cottager's diet, but the following recipe is a real Island speciality. It was originally made by Mrs. Millicent Bailey, the cook to a family who lived at Broadway, Sandown, before the last war. Mrs. Bailey was brought up in Godshill and still lives there. She kept the recipe safely so that today another Island cook, Eileen Jones, is able to bake it and sell it at Shanklin, where it is enjoyed by visitors and Islanders alike. It is the old-fashioned bread pudding you can cut into squares when cold.

GODSHILL BREAD PUDDING

1½ lbs. stale dry bread including the crusts, 4 ozs. currants, 4 ozs. sultanas, 6 ozs. suet or butter, 6 ozs. brown sugar, 3 eggs, a little milk to mix, ¼ teaspoon nutmeg, a good pinch of cinnamon, 2 ozs. finely grated orange peel, 1 tablespoon orange juice. Grease a tin that measures around twelve inches by nine inches and is about two inches deep — a meat tin is ideal. Line the bottom of the tin with thoroughly greased greaseproof paper. Soak the bread for half an hour in cold water. Put the bread into a colander and press it firmly with a draining spoon to remove any excess water. Put the bread into a mixing bowl and slake it round with a fork (an old-fashioned large-pronged fork is the best) to make it smooth. Stir in the sugar, butter, salt, fruit, spices, orange peel, and mix them well together. Beat the eggs lightly and add to the mixture with the orange juice, and milk if needed. The mixture should drop from your wooden spoon when you give it a tap on the edge of the mixing bowl. Spread the mixture evenly over the prepared tin. Bake gently at a temperature of 300F, Mark 2, for 1½–2 hours, about 1¾ hours is right. Leave the pudding in the tin to cool for several hours. Cover it with a tea towel. Turn it out carefully onto a board and peel off the greased paper. Turn it right way up and sprinkle with brown sugar and a little nutmeg while it is warm. When it is cold you can cut it into squares or it is delicious served with cream or custard. You may, of course, serve it hot with cream or custard. This recipe makes enough for twelve large portions but it keeps well in a freezer.

Godshill

This is one of my favourite sweets — very simple, very light and very nice. It is very different from the rich trifle, soaked in sherry, including crystallized fruits and almonds, that was eaten in well-to-do households. In Jane Austen's family they topped their trifle with a frothed syllabub. It is an economical attempt to copy richer recipes, ratafia essence replacing the almonds and whipped and sweetened egg whites the syllabub. It is included in a small pamphlet of Plain Cookery Recipes, published by Liverpool Training School of Cookery in 1910, price one penny.

ISLE OF WIGHT TRIFLE

3 penny sponge cakes (trifle sponges), 3 tablespoons raspberry or strawberry jam, 2 eggs with white and yolks separated, ¼ pint milk, 1 tablespoon castor sugar, 3 drops ratafia essence. Cut the sponge cakes into slices and spread them with jam; lay them in a glass dish. Make a custard* of the yolk, milk and essence, and half the sugar. Pour it over the sponge cakes and allow them to soak for a quarter of an hour. Mix the rest of the sugar with the egg whites, which must be whipped to a stiff froth, and then pile lightly on the top. Originally this trifle cost 7d (3p) to make.

*EGG CUSTARD

Half a pint of milk, one egg, one dessertspoon sugar, two or three drops vanilla essence. Beat the egg and sugar together with a fork. Heat the milk until it is very hot but not boiling. Pour it over the egg and sugar and stir the mixture well. The custard must be cooked over boiling water, in a double saucepan, or in a china basin resting on the rim of a small saucepan. Do not let the water touch the bottom of the basin. Stir the custard gently with a wooden spoon while it thickens. This takes between ten· and fifteen minutes. You must take care not to let the custard boil. The custard is ready when it coats the back of the spoon like cream.

FARMHOUSE FARE

Bacon and Beans · Casserole of Pigeons
Raised Pork Pie · Egg and Bacon Pie
Faggots · Stuffed Liver
Minced Ham with Eggs · Jellied Veal
Hasty Pudding · Marmalade Pudding
Bolton Pudding · Vectis Syrup Roll
Sunday Pudding · Pudding of the Gods
Granny Drudge's Christmas Pudding
Real Wholemeal Bread · Wheatmeal Scones
Isle of Wight Pies · Potato Tea Cakes
Isle of Wight Ginger Cake
Farmhouse Ginger Cake
Isle of Wight Doughnuts
Economical Fruit Cake
Ground Rice Biscuits
Farmhouse Christmas Cake
Elderflower Champagne · Ginger Beer
A Drink that is Nearly Equal to Bitter Beer

For its size, the Island has a surprising number of very old farmhouses, some of them dating back to the sixteenth century. Beautifully maintained, they speak of the wealth that farming created on the Island in past generations. Wheat was the golden harvest that put golden sovereigns in the Island farmers' hands.

At the end of the eighteenth century during the Napoleonic wars the Island produced an enormous amount of wheat, supplying the navy with flour and biscuit as well as providing flour and bread to the soldiers at Parkhurst barracks and in the many tented camps around the parishes. All this filled the farmers' pockets and gave them a standard of living higher than they had ever enjoyed before. The result was an out-burst of building; the old stone farmhouses in the middle and south of the Island (the most fertile land), had new fronts with nicely balanced windows on each side of the front door. Now the farmer's wife could have a dining room and parlour, with pretty cupboards where she could show off her new china and glass.

When the gentry moved out of their big sixteenth century manor houses into newly built mansions, the working farmers moved in. The manors at Mottistone, Arreton, Yaverland near Sandown, and a beautiful small manor house, West Court in Shorwell, were busy farms in the nineteenth century. Yaverland and West Court are still so today.

Inside, however smart it was to have a dining room and parlour, the living room of the farmhouse was still the kitchen, where the enormous open fireplace remained often unchanged until the nineteenth century 'Kitchener' stove filled the space. The bread oven was beside the fire and the big kitchen table stood on a flagged floor. Very few farmhouse kitchens had water brought inside but the farmer's wife and her maids could now take their water from pumps which stood near the back door and replaced the old wells. The pumps were prized possess-ions, delightfully decorated with moulded lead figures.

Amid this prosperity a rich tradition of farmhouse cooking developed on the Island. Out of this wealth I have selected some that are our favourites.

Broad beans were an important part of arable farming on the Island, growing easily on the difficult clay lands of the northern parishes, producing good crops even among weeds and requiring very little attention. Islanders dibbled the beans into the ground with a pointed stick and then left them to grow on their own. This is my method, and it works, but really good gardeners might object to all the weeds.

BACON AND BEANS

Fry your bacon until crisp. Boil the beans lightly in salted water for about 8−10 minutes if they are young − older beans need more time but I think they have a better flavour. Bring out this flavour by adding a sprig of parsley. Drain the beans and serve with the bacon and new potatoes. Delicious!

~~~~~~~

Pigeons are the farmers' bane! With so much arable land on the Island they grow so fat by late summer they can hardly launch themselves off the ground. This recipe is dated 1856.

CASSEROLE OF PIGEONS

2 pigeons split in halves, enough good stock to cover them, 6 cloves, 13 peppercorns, 12 allspice, 1 pinch mixed spice, 1 onion, sliced, salt to taste. Place all in a casserole and cook in the oven 4 hours, 275F, Mark 1−2.

The following three recipes come from the handwritten cookery book of an Island farmer's wife, Mrs. Drudge, a lady in her eighth decade. As I read through it to make my selection, little smears showed which are her favourites! It is a large book, twelve inches long by nine inches wide, carefully bound in a strong black cover and tooled in the tiniest diamond pattern all over. On the rim of the cover is a minute gold pattern tooling of leaves and scrolls. Inside, good quality lined paper has been stitched firmly into the binding. The book was made by a prisoner in Parkhurst. The farmer gave it to his young wife on the first Christmas after their wedding.

His bride evidently took the hint to heart and made her own beautifully written collection of recipes from members of her family — her mother-in-law passed on her Victorian recipes — close friends, and the journals and newspapers that came into the house, notably *The Farmer and Stockbreeder.*

RAISED PORK PIE

1½ lbs. spare rib pork, 1 onion, 1 dessertspoon powdered sage, aspic jelly, salt and pepper, 12 ozs. plain flour, 4 ozs. lard, ½ gill water, ½ gill milk. Sieve flour into a bowl, add a pinch of salt, make a well in the centre. Put milk, water, lard into a saucepan and bring to the boil. When boiling fast, pour into the flour and mix to a firm but pliable paste. Turn onto a floured board and knead for two minutes. This will help to prevent cracks from forming. Cut off a quarter of the paste for the lid, then with fingers gently spread the remainder into a round flat shape. Mould into a cup-shape over a basin or jar. Dice the pork and chop the onion. Fill with the diced pork and seasoning, mixed with the chopped onion and sprinkle over it 1½ table-spoons of water. Moisten paste lid round the edges, put it on the pie, press edges together and trim off surplus paste with scissors. Make two slits in the crust and a round hole in the centre, decorate with pastry roses and leaves. Brush the pie over with beaten egg. Place on a greased baking tin and bake in a hot oven, 375F, Mark 5, for the first fifteen minutes, then lower the heat to 300F, Mark 2, and cook for two hours. Make a stock from the pork bones and use this to make up the aspic jelly, using the quantities shown on the packet. Pour this mixture through the hole in the crust when the pie is cool. It is wise to cover the lid with two or three thicknesses of greased paper while baking.

~~~~~~~

EGG AND BACON PIE

¾ lb. short crust pastry (¾ lb. flour, 6 ozs. fat, ¼ tea-spoon salt, water to mix), ½ lb. bacon (back or streaky), ¼ lb. mushrooms, 3 eggs, pepper to taste. Knead the pastry and divide into two equal portions. Roll each into a round to fit a 9-inch pie plate. Grease the plate lightly, then line neatly with one round. Prick well with a fork. Remove rind from bacon and cut into small pieces. Arrange in pastry case. Wash, dry and slice mush-rooms on top of bacon. Beat eggs. Season with pepper to taste. Pour egg mixture over mushrooms, using a little to moisten edge of case. Cover carefully with second piece of pastry. Press edges together and crimp. Decorate centre with pastry foliage. Prick pie well and brush with beaten egg or milk. Bake in a hot oven, 400F, Mark 6, for about forty minutes.

~~~~~~~

In this recipe sage is used but you can use basil, marjoram, or any herb you wish. When the faggots, or savoury ducks as they are sometimes called, are baked in a dish, the fat from the pork pieces and the caul bind the ingredients together. Mark into squares when nearly cooked and return to the oven so that the top gets crisp. You can break them into shapes and eat them cold but I prefer them fried with fried potatoes.

FAGGOTS

½ lb. scraps of meat (pork is best), ½ lb. liver, a little lights (lungs), 4 large onions, 12 sage leaves, bread-crumbs made from ¾ of a large loaf, 4 tablespoons flour, seasoning, caul (the thin lining from a pig's stomach). Cut the ingredients very small. Chop onions and sage finely. Mix all together. Pepper and salt well. Put into pieces of caul and flour well. Bake in a medium oven, 350F, Mark 4, until nicely browned — about 80 minutes. As explained above, this mixture may be put into an enamel dish and covered with caul.

Mrs. Chessell

~~~~~~~

STUFFED LIVER

One calf's liver, sage and onion stuffing. Make an incision through the centre of the liver to the depth of half its thickness. Now put a knife into the opening and by holding it flat, cut round on each side. This will make a pocket to hold the stuffing. Bake in a hot oven, 425F, Mark 7, basting well with good dripping, for thirty minutes.

~~~~~~~

MINCED HAM WITH EGGS

Mix *½ lb. cracker crumbs with an equal quantity of finely minced lean boiled ham.* Moisten this with *stock or water and a nut of butter, adding salt to taste.* Put the mixture in a baking tin, make depressions in it the size of an egg and break *an egg* into each hollow. Bake a delicate brown in a medium—hot oven, 375F, Mark 6, for fifteen minutes.

~~~~~~~~

JELLIED VEAL

2 lbs. veal, 1 tablespoon finely chopped parsley, 1 quart water, 1 cup whipped cream, salt and pepper, 1 table-spoon gelatine, juice of ½ lemon. Cook veal at simmering point until tender. Put the meat through a mincer. Soak gelatine in ¼ cup water and add to the hot meat broth (the water in which the veal was cooked). Add minced meat and seasoning. Let mixture stand until it begins to set, then fold in whipped cream. Pour the mixture into moistened oblong container. Chill thoroughly until firm. Cut in slices and serve cold. Bony pieces of veal such as cuts from neck and shoulder are excellent.

Puddings were a really important part of a meal in the past. Here is a selection from the great variety of puddings eaten in Island farmhouses during the last three hundred years — all easy to prepare and delicious.

The first recipe is my earliest, Hasty Pudding. As the name suggests, this pudding could be put together very quickly from ingredients always to hand in the kitchen. When William King was inspired to write a cookery book in verse at the end of the seventeenth century, he included these lines about Hasty Pudding:

"Sometimes the frugal matron seems in haste
    Yet milk in proper skillet she will place,
    And gently spice it with a blade of mace:
    Into the milk her flour she gently throws . . .
    She, on the surface lumps of butter lays,
    Which, melting with the heat, its beam displays:
    From whence it causes, wondrous to behold,
    A silver soil bedeck'd with streams of gold!"

From *The Faber Book of Useful Verse*, London 1981

~~~~~~~

HASTY PUDDING
Serves two people

1 oz. butter, 1 oz. flour, 1 oz. sugar, about ¼ pt. milk. Melt the butter in a pan and add the flour, stirring to make a thick paste. Cook for about two minutes. Stir in the sugar and add sufficient milk to make a thick creamy mixture. Add the milk gradually, stirring all the time. Pour it into a dish and make small holes in the surface with the top of a wooden spoon. Drop in tiny knobs of butter and allow them to melt into "streams of gold"! This is my husband's favourite pudding.

~~~~~~~

MARMALADE PUDDING

3 tablespoons marmalade, 2 ozs. moist sugar, 1 oz. candied peel, 3 ozs. breadcrumbs, 3 ozs. flour, ¼ lb. suet, 1 lemon, 1 egg, pinch of salt. Chop the suet finely, rub the breadcrumbs through a sieve, put the flour, salt and suet into a basin and rub together with the fingers. Add the breadcrumbs, moist sugar, candied peel and marmalade, and cut the lemon in halves and squeeze the juice also into the basin. Add the egg and mix all well together. Butter a pint basin and turn the mixture into it. The basin must be full for boiling, but need not be full for steaming. Boil or steam for three and a half hours. When done turn out carefully on to a hot dish and serve with sweet sauce* or marmalade sauce.*

*SWEET SAUCE

Hasty Pudding thinned down with more milk or cream makes a delicious sweet sauce.

*MARMALADE SAUCE

2 tablespoons butter or margarine, 2 tablespoons flour or cornflour, 2 tablespoons marmalade, a little orange juice. Melt the butter gently in a pan, add the flour or cornflour gradually, stirring it until it is smooth. Add the marmalade and blend it in thoroughly. Thin the sauce down with sufficient orange juice to suit you. Serve hot in a sauce boat. Fine flour was used in the original recipe but I find cornflour gives an attractive translucent result.

The next recipe is dedicated to Thomas Orde Powlett, Lord Bolton, who was the Island Governor at the end of the eighteenth century. He lived at Fern Hill, near Wootton, but he spent the Summer months in Carisbrooke Castle, where he took a keen interest in planting trees and shrubs and in restoring the rather decayed building. One of the most pleasant remembrances we have of him today is the lovely shrubbery at the bottom of Castle Hill. During the time he was Governor, the armies of Napoleon were expected to invade England. The Island was in the front line, crammed with soldiers brought over from the mainland. There were also volunteer companies of local men armed and trained to protect their own community, who had to be specially encouraged and supported.

On the 24th June 1798, a grand gathering of the military and thousands of spectators assembled at eleven o'clock in the morning on the Bowling Green in Carisbrooke Castle to see Lord Bolton present the Isle of Wight Volunteer Corps with a new banner. It made a fine scene: the colourful uniforms of the men, the ladies in their pretty high-waisted dresses, shading their faces under deep bonnets and parasols. Most had been in the castle for some hours and had already eaten 'an elegant public Breakfast'. After the ceremony was ended the guests went on to further eating. In all, Lord Bolton entertained about four thousand people to a 'Cold Collation' — so it is only right a pudding should be named after him!

BOLTON PUDDING

3 ozs. flour, 1 oz. butter, 1½ ozs. sugar, 1 egg, 1 small teaspoon baking powder, 3 tablespoons milk, a little jam. Butter a basin and place the jam at the bottom. Rub the butter in the flour, add sugar and baking powder, mix up with the beaten egg and milk, pour into the buttered basin. Steam for one and a half hours and serve with sweet sauce (see recipe p. 33).

~~~~~~~

The next three recipes from Mrs. Drudge's book, given in their original wording, are equally simple to make, and delicious.

VECTIS SYRUP ROLL

Make a nice suet pastry with *½ lb. self-raising flour, ¼ lb. shredded suet, 2 ozs. sugar.* Mix to a stiff paste with water, roll out thinly, and spread with a mixture of *2 ozs. currants, 2 chopped apples, 2 tablespoons syrup or treacle, the grated rind of half a lemon, and a pinch of spice.* Roll up, close the edges firmly, tie in a floured cloth, and boil 2 hours.

~~~~~~~

SUNDAY PUDDING

A quarter of a pound of flour, a quarter of a pound of sugar, two ounces of butter, four eggs, one pint of milk. Beat the butter and sugar to a cream, add the flour and eggs singly. (Add the milk and beat well to make a batter mixture.) Bake in saucer tins, half full, for fifteen minutes (in a hot oven). Eat them with jam or cream.

~~~~~~~

PUDDING OF THE GODS

(Place in a glass dish) *brown breadcrumbs with a little white sugar sprinkled on them.* Upon the layer of sweetened crumbs put *whipped cream* to cover and after that *slices of apple jelly.* Repeat this until your glass dish is full. It requires no cooking.

~~~~~~~

According to tradition, Christmas Puddings should be made on 'Stir up' Sunday, so named from the collect for that Sunday in the old Book of Common Prayer which begins: "Stir up we beseech thee O Lord . . .". As this is usually about the middle of November, it is just the right time to stir up our puddings.

Labelled 'Granny Drudge' in the farmhouse book, this is a Victorian pudding passed down by word of mouth. No instructions are given with the recipe – evidently it was assumed everyone knew how to make Christmas Puddings. I will give the original recipe, then a modern version.

GRANNY DRUDGE'S CHRISTMAS PUDDING

¾ lb. flour, ¾ lb. breadcrumbs, 1 lb. suet, ¼ lb. mixed peel, ½ a nutmeg, 8 eggs, 1 lb. raisins, 1 lb. prunes, ½ lb. sugar, 1 oz. almonds, 1 lb. sultanas, pinch of salt, spice and ginger, ½ wineglass of brandy. Put into 3 greased basins, cover and boil for 5 hours and when required for 3 hours.

MODERN VERSION

6 ozs. self-raising flour, 6 ozs. fine white breadcrumbs, 8 ozs. suet, 2 ozs. mixed peel, ¼ grated nutmeg, 4 eggs, 8 ozs. raisins, 8 ozs. prunes, ¼ lb. brown sugar, 1 oz. almonds, ½ lb. sultanas, ½ teaspoon mixed spice, ½ teaspoon ground ginger, ½ wineglass brandy. Put the flour, breadcrumbs, sugar, suet and spices into a large basin and mix them together thoroughly. Chop the prunes finely and chop the almonds. Add them with the raisins, sultanas and mixed peel to the flour mixture. Beat up the eggs with the brandy and pour this over the dry ingredients, stirring the whole very well. The mixture should drop easily from the wooden spoon when it is tapped on the edge of the basin. Cover the basin with a cloth and let it stand overnight. Grease three basins and fill with the pudding mixture. Cover with greaseproof paper and then with a pudding cloth tied firmly with string. Tie the corners of the cloth together so that you make a handle for the basin. Boil for five hours, topping up occasionally with boiling water but not allowing the water to boil over the pudding. (If you steam the puddings you should allow a cooking time of 7−8 hours.) When the puddings are cooked let them get cold, then remove the greased paper and pudding cloths. Replace with fresh paper and dry cloths and store in a dry place. When required, boil them for 2−3 hours.

~~~~~~~

TEA-TIME TREATS

To make the delicious bread, scones and cakes that follow, the farmer's wife would often buy her flour direct from one of the many mills that were at work on the Island in the nineteenth century. Today, wholemeal flour is still ground at Lower Calbourne Mill, at the entrance to Newbridge village. Or, if you prefer, you can buy the flour, bread and biscuits in local shops under the trade name of 'Millers Damsel'. This is not a reference to the miller's daughter, but a description of a working part of the grinding machinery which rattles away, making sure the grain is distributed evenly between the millstones. You can hear her chattering all the time the mill is working! Less than a mile away is Upper Calbourne Mill, set in beautifully landscaped surroundings. It is open to the public and well worth a visit.

But the old recipes in this book are taken from another village mill where I can remember calling in the past. The mill is at Yafford and it is also open for all to visit. You can approach directly from the Shorwell road by the straight new drive cut through farm fields, but it is better to come across the little mill as the farmers and labourers did in the past, rounding a corner to see the

water-wheel beside the road. Yafford is a secret place
that you must look for. Signposts will direct you there
from Shorwell and from the main road that leads to
Brighstone, but Yafford is not a village or a hamlet — it
is just a neighbourhood of farms and cottages you can
pass without realizing you have been there. It is found
among narrow lanes with high banks each side, lavishly
spread over with rampant brambles, just as they were in
the nineteenth century. They are wandering lanes that
turn and twist, lanes always drawn towards the sea,
lanes made to walk in.

REAL WHOLEMEAL BREAD
Yafford, 1884

*½ lb. wholemeal flour, ½ lb. white flour (or 1 lb. whole-
meal flour if preferred), 1 teaspoon salt, 1 teaspoon
sugar, 1 teaspoon cream of tartar, 1 teaspoon carbonate
of soda, ½ pint of milk.* Mix all together, turn on to a
board well sprinkled with flour, knead lightly until there
is a smooth side underneath, place smooth side upon a
greased baking dish and bake for about ¾ hour in a hot
oven, 425—450F, Mark 7. On rapping the bottom with
the knuckles, if it gives a hollow sound it is cooked.
No yeast is needed.

~~~~~~~

WHEATMEAL SCONES

*½ lb. wheatmeal, 1 teaspoon sugar, a pinch of salt, 1 or
2 ozs. butter, 1½ teaspoons baking powder.* Mix to a
stiff paste with cream or milk; turn on to a floured
board, roll out about half an inch thick. Cut with a
round cutter, or in triangles. Bake about fifteen minutes.
Serve hot or cold with butter. I use half wholemeal and
half white flour to give a lighter mixture and bake them
at 375F, Mark 5—6. They really do need nothing but
butter on them, they are so good.

ISLE OF WIGHT PIES
Yafford, 1898

½ lb. short crust pastry, 2 eggs, 4 ozs. sugar, 4 ozs. butter, 2 large tablespoons ground rice, a few preserved cherries, a little nutmeg. Grease some patty tins and line them with thin pastry, crimp the edges and prick over the bottom with a fork; beat the eggs and sugar together until it looks thick and frothy, warm the butter and beat it with a wooden spoon until it is very soft, add the ground rice and a dust of nutmeg, and lastly the eggs and sugar; half fill the tins, place half a cherry on each, and bake in a moderate oven, 350F, Mark 4, till they are a nice brown, turn them out whilst hot, and leave on a tin until they are cold.

~~~~~~~

POTATO TEA CAKES

Boil *some nice potatoes dry,* and when cold pass them through a sieve, or mash well. Take *three ounces of mashed potatoes, three ounces of flour, one teaspoonful baking powder and a pinch of salt.* Mix all well, and then rub in lightly *three ounces of lard or dripping.* Add sufficient water to make all into a stiff paste. Roll out thin, cut with round cutters and bake at once in a hot oven until golden brown. Serve hot with butter. Sultanas or currants and a little sugar added are also liked.

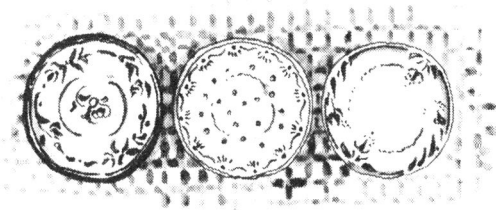

I love this recipe with its insistence on true black treacle and the picture of the oil shop it evokes with its pervasive smell of paraffin, its galvanised tins and buckets, the candles, wicks, glass lamp globes and all the other things needed in a non-electric world. You can make this cake with any good quality treacle.

ISLE OF WIGHT GINGER CAKE

Mix into *one pound of flour, a quarter of a pound of butter, one tablespoon of powdered sugar, one penny packet of baking powder (1 teaspoon), two teaspoons of powdered ginger.* Beat up and add *two eggs and a full half pound of thick treacle* — not golden syrup, but the old-fashioned treacle sold at oil shops. You may need to thin the treacle with a little milk before you can work it in. Beat all well together, and bake for two hours in a slow (cool) oven, 275F, Mark 1—2.

~~~~~~~

FARMHOUSE GINGER CAKE

Heat together *2 tablespoons brown sugar, 2 tablespoons margarine, 1 tablespoon golden syrup, 1 tablespoon black treacle* until they are thoroughly warm. Beat *two eggs in a small cup of milk* and add to the ingredients in the pan. Add *2 teacups of flour, a pinch of salt, 1 teaspoon mixed spice, 2 teaspoons ground ginger, 1 teaspoon carbonate of soda.* Mix all well together. Put into a greased tin and bake in a moderate oven (350—375F, Mark 3—4) for about 45 minutes. This recipe was found in an old farmhouse.

This old recipe describes in detail how to make a favourite Island tea-time treat. Unlike ordinary doughnuts the Island variety have no jam but include currants and candied peel.

A visit to Newport market was not complete without calling at Westmore's Doughnut Shop, on the corner of Scarrot's Lane and Upper St. James's Street. When the market was held in St. James's Square this little shop was just convenient for a cup of tea and a doughnut at the end of a day's shopping. Recently I met the granddaughter of Mrs. Westmore who told me the shop was always packed with people from the country. She also said that the doughnuts were smaller than those we eat today, so that the size given in the following recipe — about that of a small orange — was followed.

Today, you can still buy Isle of Wight doughnuts in Newport and so, if you are feeling nostalgic or just want to try an Island doughnut, you should make your way to Eric's in Nodehill, or to Wray's at the top of the High Street, and take some home for tea. Or try making some yourself. I quote the original quantities — reduce the amounts to manageable proportions.

ISLE OF WIGHT DOUGHNUTS

One gallon of flour (10 lbs.), one pound of butter rubbed well into it: pour in *one teacupful of good ale yeast* (not bitter) and put it to rise; mix and knead it as you would bread, add *six well-beaten eggs, three quarters of a pound of sifted sugar, one grated nutmeg, and a little warm milk.* The dough must not be mixed too soft at first, or it will be too soft to roll up subsequently. Leave it again by the fire to rise for an hour or two. Then take out small lumps of dough, the size of a smallish orange, insert into the centre of each *a piece of candied peel and some currants (some grated lemon rind also is a great improvement)*; roll it up securely. Have ready a deep pan of quite boiling lard (any fat or oil suitable for deep frying) and be sure that it is quite boiling when the doughnuts are put in: let them be completely covered with the lard, and boil fifteen minutes over a slow fire (flame or burner). Take out, set to drain on paper, and let them cool gradually and not stand in a draught. Dust over with sifted sugar. These are first-rate.

~~~~~~~~

During the last war the members of the Women's Institutes were busy helping with the war effort. In Carisbrooke this included making pounds of blackberry jam in the old kitchen at Priory Farm, which stands just behind the parish church. Impromptu recipes included Carrot Cookies and Prune Cake! In Mrs. Drudge's book I found a recipe for an eggless, boiled cake which was made during the war years. Eggless cake was part of wartime life and recipes for boiled cakes were popular because the fruit swelled and the cake gained moisture from the boiling process. But this is a delicious cake, a nice brown in colour, spicy and moist. One five-year-old visitor of mine tried a piece and came back for three more, saying it was the best cake she had ever tasted.

ECONOMICAL FRUIT CAKE

Put into a saucepan: *1 cup brown sugar, 1 cup water, 1½ cups fruit (various), ½ or one-third cup of lard or butter, a few gratings of nutmeg, ½ teaspoon of cinnamon, ½ teaspoon of mixed spice, pinch of salt.* Boil together for three minutes. When nearly cold add *1 teaspoon carbonate of soda dissolved in hot water and 2 cups of flour into which ½ teaspoon baking powder* has been sifted. Mix well and bake in a warm oven, 300F, Mark 2–3, for 1½ hours.

~~~~~~~~

GROUND RICE BISCUITS

Three ounces of butter, three ounces of white sugar, six ounces of ground rice, three ounces of flour, half a teaspoonful of baking powder, one egg (beaten), a little milk, grated lemon rind. Cream the butter and sugar, then add the egg and dry ingredients. The mixture should be like pastry; turn onto a floured board, roll lightly (as it will stick), and cut into biscuits a quarter of an inch thick. Place on a greased tin; bake in a moderate oven, 300–325F, Mark 3, to a golden brown.

~~~~~~~

This recipe was attributed to 'Gran' in Mrs. Drudge's book and is a marvellous example of the very rich recipes used for special cakes in Victorian times. It is just as good today and you can either bake it in one large tin or two smaller ones.

FARMHOUSE CHRISTMAS CAKE

1 lb. butter, 1 lb. castor sugar, 1 lb. flour, 8 eggs (yolks and whites separated), 4 ozs. almonds, ½ lb. mixed peel, 3 lbs. currants, wineglass sherry, wineglass brandy. Blanch almonds 2 hours before using and then cover them with the brandy until required. Beat the butter and sugar to a cream. Add the eggs gradually, then the currants, peel, and almonds, with the sherry. Mix well and then add the flour, stirring it in very gently. This should be cooked in a well-greased tin that has been lined with greaseproof paper. Bake 4½ hours at 325F or Mark 3. To see if the cake is cooked, insert a thin skewer into the cake after 4 hours. If it comes out clean the cake is cooked. Allow to cool in the tin for about 30 minutes and then turn out.

~~~~~~~

ELDERFLOWER CHAMPAGNE

2 heads of elderflowers, 1 gallon of water, 1¼ lbs. sugar, few tablespoons white wine vinegar. Mix all the ingredients together and leave covered for 24 hours. Strain the liquid and put into bottles with screw tops. Leave for a minimum of 2−3 weeks, but for the best results leave for 6 months.

Bob Fewtrell

~~~~~~~~

The following recipes for drinks were found while turning out cupboards in an old farmhouse. They were written on small sheets of thick paper, now beige-brown with age, and the handwriting shows that they belong to the early years of the nineteenth century. I have set them out as they are written with my own notes in brackets.

GINGER BEER

Put in a pan *1 lb. Sugar, 10 ozs. Cream Tartar, 1 oz. Ground Ginger.* Pour on *1 gallon boiling water.* Stir well. When milk-warm, put *a piece of toasted bread with Barm (yeast) spread both sides,* on the top. Next day take the bread gently off and put (the liquid) in a jar. It is ready for use.

~~~~~~~~

A DRINK THAT IS NEARLY EQUAL TO BITTER BEER

To four ozs. Hops and five Gallons of Water (add) four ozs. Bruised Ginger. Boil all together an hour and a half, add more water as it boils away. Then strain in a pan. Put *6 lbs. Sugar (to it),* stir well. When nearly cold, stir in *half a cup of barm (yeast).* Let it stand to work a few days then put in a jar or bottles.

44

AN ISLAND STORE CUPBOARD

Yaverland Apple Jelly
Blackberry and Apple Jelly
Quince Jelly
Gooseberry Jam with Elder Flowers
Old-fashioned Raspberry Jam
Quick Raspberry Jam
Blackcurrant and Raspberry Jam
Northcourt Cherry Jam
Victorian Marrow and Ginger Jam
Lemon Cheese
Orange Marmalade

Apple Chutney
Tomato Chutney
Tomato Honey
Farmhouse Tomato Chutney
St. Dominic's Japanese Quince Chutney
St. Dominic's Apple Devil
Victorian Pickled Red Cabbage

In the past, the occupants of most Island homes, from the humblest cottage to Osborne House itself, relied heavily on a well-stocked store cupboard to help them through the long winter months. The Island is still a rural community and the business of preserving is an important part of our lives. And what satisfaction it brings to see a full store cupboard with rows of neatly arranged jams, jellies and chutneys!

Towards the end of September my small kitchen is crammed – marrows sit on the washing machine, windfall apples are in boxes on the floor, tomatoes are piled in dishes on the work bench, and mountains of plums await me, all seeming to need my attention immediately. But it is such a pleasure to fill my store cupboard with these time-honoured Island specialities.

John Smith of Yaverland kept very detailed account books in which he entered the wages he paid his labourers, his buying and selling prices for produce, how much he paid in Poor Rates, Church Tithe, and other taxes. Among all these economic details was slipped in this little recipe which was obviously a favourite to have found its way into a farm diary. It is very richly flavoured, being made from pure juice only, and it sets firmly.

YAVERLAND APPLE JELLY
Yaverland, 1836

"Let the apples be pared, quartered, and freed from seed vessels, put them in an oven, in a pot without water, with a close lid. When the heat has made them soft, put them into a cloth, and wring out the juice. Put a little white of Egg into it. Add a little sugar. Skim it carefully before it boils. Reduce it to a proper consistency and you will have an excellent Jelly."

From John Smith's account book, Yaverland, *c*. 1836

MODERN VERSION

Prepare the apple pulp as John Smith suggests and put it into a jelly bag or clean cloth and leave it to drip overnight. *A white of egg* stirred in helps to clarify the apple juice. *To each pint of juice add 1 lb. preserving or granulated sugar* (remember to warm the sugar first). Allow the sugar to dissolve completely and then boil briskly for 20—25 minutes. Skim off any froth. To test for setting, drop a little of the jelly onto a really cold plate. Push the jelly gently with your little finger. It should crinkle up and remain like that. Always remove the pan from the heat while you do this, so that the jelly does not overcook. Jam jars must be clean, dry and warm when they are filled.

~~~~~~~~~

BLACKBERRY AND APPLE JELLY

4 lbs. blackberries, 4 lbs. apples, 1 pt. water, 1 lb. sugar to each pint of juice. Boil the fruit one hour in water. Strain or drip overnight. Reheat juice, allow 1 lb. sugar to each pint and simmer until the sugar has dissolved. Boil rapidly for 10 minutes or until jelly wrinkles when touched with the finger (remember to put a small amount of jelly on a saucer to do this).

~~~~~~~~

Quince trees thrive in the mild, sunny climate of the Island. They are a very old fruit, eaten in noble families in the Middle Ages, when they were called 'quoins'.

QUINCE JELLY

2½ lbs. windfall apples or crab apples, 2 lbs. quinces, 1 lb. sugar for each pint of juice, rind and juice of two lemons. Peel and slice the quinces. Wash the apples or crabs and cut them to an even size. Put the fruit in a preserving pan and cover them with enough water to float them. Boil until the fruit is reduced to a pulp. Put into a jelly bag or cloth and let it drip overnight. Add one pound of sugar to each pint of liquid, together with the lemon juice and thin peelings of rind. Bring gently to the boil and boil for about 40 minutes until the jelly is ready to set. Skim off any scum and the rinds. Pour into warm jars.

~~~~~~~~

GOOSEBERRY JAM WITH ELDER FLOWERS

3 lbs. green gooseberries, 1 pt. water, 4 lbs. preserving sugar, 3 large elder flower heads. Simmer the fruit in water until tender, about 25 minutes. Add the warmed sugar and allow it to dissolve. Bring to the boil and add the elder flowers tied in muslin. Let them stay in the jam for three to four minutes, then remove them (elder flowers have such a strong aroma that you need only draw a bunch of heads through the jam when it is finished boiling to give it a delicate flavour). Test for setting after ten minutes boiling. Skim the jam and pour into warm dry jars.

~~~~~~~

OLD-FASHIONED RASPBERRY JAM

6 lbs. raspberries, 6 lbs. preserving sugar. Place the fruit in a large basin and stand the basin over a pan of boiling water. Crush the fruit with a wooden spoon. When quite soft, add hot sugar and stir until the sugar is dissolved. Turn into a preserving pan and boil for ten minutes. Bottle as usual.

~~~~~~~

QUICK RASPBERRY JAM

Allow 1¼ lbs. preserving sugar for each pound of raspberries. Put the fruit into a preserving pan and heat slowly until the juice runs, then bring to the boil. Boil for no more than 2−3 minutes. Lower the heat and add the warmed sugar, stirring until it completely dissolves. Bring quickly to the boil and remove immediately from the heat. Put into warm dry jars. I have kept this jam successfully for well over a year.

~~~~~~~

BLACKCURRANT AND RASPBERRY JAM

Take *3 lbs. of blackcurrants* that have been stalked and cleaned. Put them into a preserving pan with *2 lbs. of raspberries and about half a pint of water.* Cook until the blackcurrants are soft. Then add *sugar in proportion of ¾ lb. to every pound of fruit.* Let the sugar dissolve and then boil rapidly until it will set nicely if a little is tested on a plate. Put into pots and cover. This is a delicious flavoured jam, preferable to redcurrant mixture.

~~~~~~~

This recipe for Morello Cherry Jam came to me from Mrs. Miriam Harrison, who lives at Northcourt, one of the largest and most beautiful manor houses on the Island. It stands in Shorwell near the church at the bottom of a steep wooded shute that leads the road from Newport into the village. The manor grounds include an eighteenth century walled garden in which vegetables and fruit grow in ordered patterns.

NORTHCOURT CHERRY JAM

6 lbs. Morello cherries, 6 lbs. preserving sugar, ¾ pint redcurrant juice. Cook the cherries gently in a little water to soften them so that you can take out the stones. Put the stoned fruit into a preserving pan. Crack a few of the stones, take out the kernels and blanch them in boiling water. Add these to the cherries, together with the remaining stones tied in a muslin bag. Add the currant juice with the warmed sugar. Heat gently until the sugar has completely dissolved, then boil rapidly until the jam sets. Turn into warm jars and cover when cold. Gooseberry juice is an alternative to help the jam to set or you could use a commercial pectin such as Certo.

~~~~~~~

This Victorian recipe comes from Mrs. Drudge's cookery book. Only really ripe marrows should be used for jam making. The jam must be boiled gently for a long time — sometimes more than two hours — in order to get the transparent consistency. If it is boiled too quickly it will become sugary and crystalline.

VICTORIAN MARROW AND GINGER JAM

4 lbs. marrow (weighed after paring and coring), 3 lbs. sugar, 1 tablespoon vinegar, 2 good-sized lemons (grated rinds and juice), 2 ozs. root ginger, well-bruised and tied in a cloth. Cut the marrow into pieces the size of lump sugar and allow the sugar to stand on it overnight. Put all into a preserving pan with the vinegar, lemon rind and juice, and the ginger. Boil until clear — about 1½ hours. It boils down a good deal.

~~~~~~~

I asked the champion Lemon Cheese maker in our County Federation of Women's Institutes how she kept on producing superb results year after year. Mrs. Joliffe told me that the lemon peel must be grated on the finest possible grater and the cheese must be cooked over boiling water. A double saucepan is ideal but I have had quite high marks in our W.I. competition for my Lemon Cheese using a basin fitted tightly to the rim of a saucepan, making certain it did not touch the water below.

LEMON CHEESE

Put into a saucepan *half a pound of castor sugar, two beaten eggs, three ounces of butter, and the juice and grated rind of a lemon.* Bring it to the boil slowly, until it looks thick (like honey), then put into jars and cover down. This is used for filling open tarts and cheese cakes.

~~~~~~~

ORANGE MARMALADE

To 3 lbs. of oranges in their skins allow 6 lbs. lump sugar, or preserving sugar. Wash and brush the oranges, put them in a stewpan with sufficient boiling water to float them and boil slowly for ¼ hour. Pour that water away and add more boiling water, and boil slowly until a straw will pierce them easily. Cut in halves, remove pips, scoop out the insides. Cut the rind into thin chips. Save a pint of the last water in which the oranges were boiled. Put the orange peel and pulp, the water and warm sugar back into the preserving pan. Set over a low heat until the sugar has dissolved. Add the pips tied in a muslin bag and when the marmalade comes to the boil simmer for half an hour, stirring gently all the time. Test for setting. Remove the bag of pips, pressing it against the side of the pan to squeeze out the pectin. Fill hot dry jars to the brim. Cover with a greased paper disc, and then with a cellophane top. This marmalade is excellent. The addition of the water in which the oranges were boiled gives it an extra tang.

APPLE CHUTNEY

20 apples, 1 lb. raisins (seeded), 1 lb. sugar, 1 lb. onions, ¾ pint vinegar, ¼ oz. mustard seed, ¼ oz. cayenne pepper, 1 or 2 cloves. Peel, core and slice the apples. Boil them with the onions in vinegar until they are soft. Add all the remaining ingredients and boil for a few minutes. When the mixture looks thick, fill the pots.

~~~~~~~

FARMHOUSE TOMATO CHUTNEY

3 lbs. green tomatoes, 3 large apples, ½ lb. sultanas, ¼ lb. shallots, 1 lb. demerara sugar, 1½ pints vinegar, a little whole ginger, pepper and a few chillies. Cut up the tomatoes and shallots. Sprinkle them with salt and leave all night. Strain off the salt liquid. Put the tomatoes, shallots and the other ingredients into a large pan and cook for 2—3 hours. Put into warm dry jars and cover.

~~~~~~~

TOMATO HONEY

1 lb. tomatoes, 1 orange (rind and juice), 1 lemon (rind and juice), sugar. Note: 1 lb. of firm tomatoes makes about ½ pint of purée, softer tomatoes would make more. Chop up the tomatoes. Peel the orange and lemon rind thinly. Cook the tomatoes and rind in a saucepan until soft. Put the mixture through a sieve and measure. For every pint allow 1 lb. sugar. Add the orange and lemon juice and simmer until it is the consistency of honey. Put into small, warm, dry pots and cover.

~~~~~~~

TOMATO CHUTNEY

4 lbs. green tomatoes, 1 large onion, ½ oz. mustard, ½ lb. brown sugar, 6 apples, ½ oz. pepper, ¼ oz. ground ginger, ½ teaspoon allspice, 3 pints vinegar, salt. Slice the tomatoes and onion very thinly. Sprinkle salt over the layers and leave 24 hours, then drain. Add pepper, mustard, ginger, sugar and allspice, cover well with the vinegar and simmer in an enamel saucepan until tender. (This can take up to 1½ hours, but thorough boiling is necessary so that a thick, rich mixture results. It should drop easily from a spoon.) Add the six apples, peeled, cored and chopped, when the chutney is half-cooked — after about half an hour. Put into warm dry jars and cover. This chutney can be eaten soon after it is made.

From our cottage window we can see the outline of St. Dominic's Priory on the skyline, a wonderful sight at sunset, when the steep-pitched roof and Gothic bell tower are etched in black against the western sky. Forced to leave their convent in Belgium after the outbreak of the Napoleonic wars, this community of Dominican nuns had no settled home until the Dowager Countess of Clare built this Priory for them on the hill above Carisbrooke in 1866. The sisters are great gardeners and very good cooks. I am grateful to them for the next two recipes, which are particularly nice. Japanese quinces are the fruit of the tree with scarlet flowers, often grown in our gardens, called *Chaenomeles japonica.* They flourish in the garden of St. Dominic's.

ST. DOMINIC'S JAPANESE QUINCE CHUTNEY

4 lbs. apples (windfalls are suitable), 2 lbs. Japanese quinces, ½ lb. brown sugar, 1 pt. spiced vinegar,* ½ lb. green tomatoes, cayenne pepper to taste, 1 tablespoon salt. Core and chop the apples and quinces, add sugar and sliced green tomatoes. Sprinkle with a tablespoon of salt and a pinch of cayenne pepper (if liked). Cover with the spiced vinegar. Simmer gently for two hours, stirring frequently. Put into jars and cover tightly.

*SPICED VINEGAR

1 pint vinegar, ½ oz. peppercorns, ½ oz. root ginger, ½ oz. allspice. Bruise the spices and put them in a muslin bag. Add to the vinegar, bring to the boil and let them simmer, covered, for about 8 minutes. Let the spices remain in the vinegar until quite cold. Strain and use as directed.

~~~~~~~

ST. DOMINIC'S APPLE DEVIL

Peel and core about *30 good cooking apples* and slice them into *a little cold water.* Add *equal weight lump sugar, the juice and peel of two lemons cut very thin, 2 ozs. of very finely grated ginger, and 1 teaspoon cayenne pepper.* Boil all together until the apples look quite clear. The quantity of cayenne can be diminished to suit the taste. This will keep for 2—3 years and is eaten as a preserve.

~~~~~~~~

VICTORIAN PICKLED RED CABBAGE

Dated 1823, I give this recipe in its original wording, but it is not difficult to follow today: Slice into a colander and sprinkle each layer of *cabbage* with *salt,* let it drain for 2 days, then put it into a stoneware jar, pour *boiling vinegar* enough to cover, and put in *a few slices of red beetroot.* Observe to choose the purple red cabbage. Those who like the flavour of spices will boil some with the vinegar. Cauliflower cut in small bunches and thrown in after being salted with the sliced cabbage will look a beautiful red.

~~~~~~~~

FOOD FIT FOR GENTLEMEN

Cowes Pudding
Sandown Pudding
Mountain Pudding
Gooseberry Fool
Everlasting Syllabub
Solid Syllabub
Stuffed Pork
Onion and Kidney Savoury
Tomato and Mushroom Savoury

Victorian Ground Rice Biscuits
Jumbles
Dr. Williamson's Christmas Cake
A Yacht Steward's Mayonnaise
Boiled Ham

Victorian Cheese Pudding
Quick Cheese Pudding
Macaroni Cheese
Savoury Rice with Cheese
Cheese Straws

The Island was a country of gentlemen. Not great aristocrats with widely spread estates but men of comfortable means who lived at home most of the year, settled on their land, closely involved in local life and inextricably connected through marriage with the other gentry families in the Island.

In the eighteenth century they built the elegant country houses we see today: Northwood House at Cowes, the home of the Ward family; Farringford at Freshwater, a pretty Gothic building that was later enlarged when the Tennysons went to live there; Norris Castle at East Cowes, the eighteenth century 'medieval' castle built by James Wyatt, romantic and perfectly placed overlooking the Solent; and Westover House at Calbourne, which retains all the elegance of the Regency period with its curving bows and classical pediment. Richard Worsley built the finest house of all, Apple-durcombe. Now it is only a ruin but even as it stands, roofless and windowless, its grey stone walls austere against the sky, the great beauty of its design remains.

The gentry managed all forms of local administration and were expected to take a charitable interest in the poor. A picture of what this meant in one Island Rectory was left by the son of the Rector of Whippingham, Roland Prothero. He was growing up in the 1850s and 60s, and he remembered that each Sunday after morning service his father came into the servants' hall and carved slices off a sirloin of beef to form Sunday dinner for half-a-dozen or so old people in the neighbourhood. Roland's duty was to add a large baked potato to each portion before the dishes were carried out.

These country houses were remarkably self-sufficient. At Whippingham Rectory they supplied their own milk, eggs, poultry, fruit, and vegetables, and brewed their own beer. Groceries were sent down from London, the butcher called once a week for orders, and fresh fish came from Cowes.

An important change took place in the eating and serving of meals. In the eighteenth century dinner in the middle of the afternoon was the single main meal, with only a very light breakfast and a small supper between nine and ten o'clock. Gradually, the pattern changed. Dinner moved to the evening and, from being a meal where all the dishes were set out together on the table, during Queen Victoria's reign it became one in which separate courses of particular dishes were brought on in regular order.

Puddings were still an important feature at dinner parties. It is interesting to see how much almond was used as a flavouring for these elegant dishes.

COWES PUDDING

½ pint milk, 2 eggs, ¼ lb. savoy biscuits, 2 ozs. almonds, 2 tablespoons of castor sugar, ½ oz. butter, a few drops of almond essence. Sauce: *The yolks of three eggs, 1 tablespoon of castor sugar, ¼ pint sherry.* Grease the basin with the butter, blanch the almonds, skin them and chop them finely, beat up the two eggs with sugar, boil the milk and make custard (see p. 24) with the eggs. Line the basin with the biscuits cut in half. Add the almonds with the essence to the custard, then pour into the basin; it must be full. Cover with paper and steam ¾ hour. When done let it stand a minute before turning out, then turn out and pour the sauce round. To make the sauce, put all the ingredients (the egg yolks, castor sugar and sherry) into a saucepan, whisk them over heat until thick, but they must not boil.

~~~~~~~

SANDOWN PUDDING

Butter a cake tin and line it with *sponge fingers or boudoir biscuits.* Put in *two ounces of glacé cherries and two ounces of ratafias.* Make *a pint of custard* (see p. 24) and add to it *three ounces of gelatine.* Pour into a mould or tin, leave it to cool and serve as a cold pudding with whipped cream.

~~~~~~~

MOUNTAIN PUDDING

Butter a pie dish and line it with *ratafias*; grate *the rind of a lemon* over them. Mix *two ounces of flour with a little cold milk* to a smooth paste, and *add cold milk* gradually to make a pint; boil this for ten minutes, stirring all the time. Stir in *the yolks of two eggs.* Pour the mixture gently over the ratafias and leave them to soak for ten minutes. Beat *the whites of the two eggs* to a stiff froth, stir *two ounces of castor sugar* to this, and add *a little cornflour or arrowroot* to make the icing stiff. Arrange it on the pudding in four or five little mounds, and put the pudding in the oven till these are slightly brown. Serve cold. The icing will take no harm if made two or three hours before it is wanted.

~~~~~~~

TO MAKE A GOOSEBERRY FOOL

This recipe is dated 1662 and I quote it in its original wording with my notes in brackets: Take your *Gooseberries,* and put them in a Silver or Earthen Pot (a bowl that will not crack) and set it in a Skillet (large saucepan) of boyling water, and when they are coddled enough (softened) strain them, then make them hot again, when that they are scalding hot, beat them very well with *a good piece of fresh butter, Rose-water* and Sugar* (to taste), and put in *the yolke of two or three Eggs*; you may put Rose-water into them and so stir it altogether, and serve it to the Table when it is cold. Note: the gooseberries can be very gently simmered with a very little water and then sieved before reheating them and continuing with the recipe.

* You can buy Rose-water in any good chemist or health food shop.

~~~~~~~

Syllabubs were a favourite cream pudding, especially enjoyed in the eighteenth century. With jellies, they formed the centrepiece of the dinner table, with other dishes set around them. They are splendid for a dinner party today. This is an excellent syllabub and with an electric or rotary beater it is quick to make. It is essential to have the cream thick. The mixture separates out while it is standing so that the wine settles at the bottom of the glass. When you begin to eat the syllabub the wine percolates through the cream. This amount will fill eight wine glasses.

EVERLASTING SYLLABUB

Steep *the peel and juice of one lemon* overnight in *a wineglassful of white wine.* Next morning pour this into a deep pan, and stir in gradually *half a pint of thick cream with sugar to taste.* Whip for a quarter of an hour − or until really thick − and put into glasses. This is better made the day before eating and it will keep for several days.

~~~~~~~

SOLID SYLLABUB
Bowcombe, 1854

This is even easier and quicker and, as its name suggests, the cream remains solid. You will have enough to fill twelve wine glasses. Squeeze *the juice of one lemon into half a pint of sherry.* Grate *the peel over ¼ lb. loaf sugar.* Stir into the sherry until the sugar is melted, add *1 pint thick cream* and beat until the mixture is quite thick, then fill your glasses. Grate *a little nutmeg* on top of each.

~~~~~~~

In the past, this recipe was eaten as a breakfast dish; now it makes an excellent main course. Breakfast was a really substantial meal for our ancestors, who had generally done at least an hour's work before they stopped to eat. The country squire did not stop for lunch. Weekly meetings of the Guardians of the Poor at Newport began at twelve noon and magistrates sat well into the afternoon. Country gentlemen expected to ride round their land, to shoot or hunt during the season, in the time between breakfast and dinner. At home their wives used the time for morning and afternoon visits and for work in the parish, stopping for only a slice or two of cold meat to stave off hunger until dinner time.

STUFFED PORK

Take *two pounds of streaky green pork* (the thinner the better) and *one pound of sausage meat.* Spread the sausage meat on the underside of the pork, covering one half; now fold the other half over, bind with strips of calico (or any strips of cloth), and simmer steadily for about two hours. When cooked, press between two plates.

~~~~~~~

ONION AND KIDNEY SAVOURY

Grease a fireproof dish. Take *a spanish onion,* cut out the centre, insert *a kidney* which has been washed and skinned. Bake in a hot oven, 375F, Mark 5, basting frequently with cooking butter, for 35 minutes. Serve with a thick brown gravy.

~~~~~~~

TOMATO AND MUSHROOM SAVOURY

This is best if you are able to use the big field or 'horse' mushrooms, which can easily cover a slice of bread. The savoury looks very attractive as well as tasting good. Cut as many *rounds of bread* as you require, *butter them and place a mushroom (or mushrooms)* upon each. On the mushroom place *a tomato which has been peeled, season with salt and pepper,* and bake in a medium—hot oven for about ten minutes, 340—370F, Mark 4—5.

'An Outdoor meal at Steepe Hill' by John Nixon reproduced by permission of the Trustees of Carisbrooke Castle Museum from a watercolour presented to the Museum collection by the Friends of the Museum.

Queen Victoria dined at eight in the evening and fashionable society followed her lead. Afternoon Tea at five o'clock came into being to bridge the gap and reached its heyday in the 1890s. It was essentially a dainty meal, served in the drawing room or even the Hall in country houses. A small table was covered with a fine white cloth, lavishly decorated with a lace edging and laid with delicate bone china. Equally decorative was the mistress of the house in her elegant tea-gown, as she poured tea from her silver service and exchanged polite conversation with her friends. The tiny sandwiches, cakes and biscuits also handed round would include the following recipes.

VICTORIAN GROUND RICE BISCUITS

Three ounces of butter, three ounces of white sugar, six ounces of ground rice, three ounces of flour, half a teaspoon baking powder, one egg (beaten), a little milk, grated lemon rind. Cream the butter and sugar, then add the beaten egg and dry ingredients. The mixture should be like pastry; turn on to a floured board, roll lightly (as it is likely to stick), and cut into biscuits a quarter of an inch thick. Place on a greased tin and bake in a hot oven, 375F, Mark 5, to a golden brown — about fifteen to twenty minutes.

JUMBLES

4 ozs. butter, 6 ozs. sugar, 8 ozs. plain flour, 1 large egg. Beat the butter and sugar to a light creamy consistency. Add the egg. Fold in the flour. The resulting paste will be very soft. Take off small knobs about the size of a walnut. Roll them on a floured board, or between your hands, into strips about 3 inches long. Have ready a greased baking sheet. Make the strips into 'S' shapes and lay them on the sheet, leaving room for them to spread. Bake in a moderate oven, 375F, Mark 5, for fifteen minutes until the jumbles are golden brown. Let them cool for a few minutes and then lift on to a wire tray.

This cake was made each year in the home of a Ventnor doctor, Bruce Williamson. He was himself the son of a doctor who practised from the same house during the nineteenth century. Among the elder doctor's patients were Karl Marx and Winston Churchill! Marx consulted him towards the end of his life and Churchill was brought to see him at the beginning of his.

DR. WILLIAMSON'S CHRISTMAS CAKE

½ lb. butter, ½ lb. sugar (granulated or soft brown), ¾ lb. self-raising flour, 2 lbs. fruit (sultanas and stoneless raisins), 3 eggs, ½ teaspoon vanilla essence, ½ teaspoon almond essence, 2 ozs. cherries, wineglass of sherry, a little milk. Crumble the butter into the flour, add the sugar, then the eggs. Put in the fruit and mix well. Finally, add the sherry and flavourings. Put thick layers of greaseproof paper (or foil) inside the tin before adding the cake mixture. The tin should be greased with lard. Cook for three hours at 325F, Mark 3, and leave the cake to cool in the tin.

MARZIPAN PASTE

¾ lb. ground almonds, ½ lb. icing sugar, a few drops of almond essence, one or two egg yolks. Mix the almonds and sugar well with a wooden spoon, and add sufficient egg yolk to make a smooth, workable paste. Pound the mixture lightly to release a little of the almond oil. Brush the surface of the cake with a little *hot apricot jam.* This will make the marzipan paste stick to the cake.

Many years before Queen Victoria made her home at Osborne, the little harbour town of Cowes was attracting the aristocracy during the sailing season. In 1801 a local newspaper reported that visitors made sailing their chief diversion and that "water pick-nicks" were popular. In 1815 the first step that was to make Cowes supreme in the yachting world was taken when some of the gentry met to form the Yacht Club, later to be called the Royal Yacht Club and finally, in 1833, the Royal Yacht Squadron.

The heyday of luxury came at the end of the century when steam yachts were the status symbol of wealth and fashion and the Prince of Wales visited Cowes regularly. The steam yachts were elegant and graceful, with their long bowsprits emphasizing the sweeping lines of the hull, and below decks they were floating palaces. Corinthian pillars supported the plaster ceilings of saloons panelled with polished mahogany or varnished oak, featuring elaborate carved fireplaces with mirrors above them, and furnished with velvet-covered chairs and settees. The dining salon followed the same style, with polished tables, sideboards, white damask tablecloths, crystal glass, and delicate dinner services. This was the yacht steward's province.

A YACHT STEWARD'S MAYONNAISE

Whisk *the yolk of six eggs,* add to them *one dessertspoon of made mustard, one saltspoon salt, and a pinch of cayenne,* stirring all the time. Put them into an enamel saucepan, then add *a quarter of a pint of salad oil,* whisking all the time; next, *a quarter of a pint of milk or cream, one tablespoon of vinegar, and the same of Worcester sauce.* Last, add *a quarter of a pint of vinegar.* Continue to stir gently all the time you are mixing, or the sauce will curdle. Now put the saucepan over a slow fire (burner) and whisk until it becomes thick. It must not boil. Take it off the fire (burner), continue stirring gently until it cools. Then put it into wide-mouthed bottles, cork closely, and it will keep for two or three months. This is a yacht steward's recipe and most excellent.

~~~~~~~~

It is interesting to compare this luxury with the food a modern sailor, Uffa Fox, thought suitable for cruising. A practical and experienced seaman, he is as sensible in his choice of provisions, preferring "soups and stews and all sorts of wholesome food . . .". (From *According to Uffa*, Newnes, London, 1960.) He liked to take with him a boiled ham to provide a nourishing grease-free breakfast for his crew while they were finding their sea legs.

BOILED HAM

If you can soak your *gammon joint* overnight, do so, but failing this, put it in cold water, bring it to the boil, then pour away the water. Put the gammon into a large saucepan and cover with cold water. Peel and slice *2 potatoes, 2 carrots, 2 onions* and add them to the ham with *6 peppercorns.* Bring it slowly to the boil and simmer gently. Allow 20–25 minutes per pound. You can tell when it is ready if the fat peels away easily from the meat when you insert a sharp pointed knife. If you are to eat the joint cold, let it cool in the water so that it does not lose any moisture.

Cheese dishes were popular on the Island but we can be quite certain none of them was ever made from Isle of Wight cheese! Not even the paupers in the House of Industry in Newport would eat it — their cheese was bought at regular fairs in Hampshire and imported. Island cheese was universally known as Isle of Wight Rock. Island farmers concentrated on the production of cream and butter, so only skimmed milk was left for cheese making, hence the disastrous results. Two stories, both connected with the transportation of these great round cheeses, have been retold for generations on the Island. When cheese and mill-stones were stored in the hold of a ship, the rats preferred to chew the stones, and when storms threatened a ship with the same cargo, the Island cheese was thrown overboard first to lighten the load! An agricultural writer summed up the quality of this remarkable cheese in the 1790s — "it can scarcely be cut by a hatchet or saw; is to be masticated only by the firmest teeth and digested only by the strongest stomachs". And yet somebody ate it, as they were still making Isle of Wight Rock on farms in the south of the Island in the 1860s.

VICTORIAN CHEESE PUDDING

Put into a bowl ¼ *lb. breadcrumbs* and pour over this *½ pint boiling milk*. Let it stand for half an hour. Beat well and add *1 oz. butter, ¼ lb. grated cheese, 2 well-beaten eggs, mustard, salt and pepper to taste.* Put in a well-greased basin. Steam for 1¼ hours and serve with cheese or tomato sauce. This makes an excellent supper dish.

QUICK CHEESE PUDDING

Two ounces of grated cheese, two ounces of bread-crumbs, one ounce of butter, one teaspoon made mustard, half a gill of milk, one egg, cayenne pepper, salt. Put butter and milk into a saucepan, make quite hot, pour it over the mixed crumbs and cheese, then add the yolk of the egg and mustard, mixed. Whip white of egg and add lastly, or it may be piled on top (when the pudding is cooked) with a little grated cheese, and just set. Bake the pudding twenty minutes in a medium oven, 300F, Mark 2—3.

~~~~~~~

The next recipe contains curry powder and Roland Prothero recalled how this was brought to the Rectory at Whippingham and other Island homes in the late 1850s, by a "little shrivelled old man, dressed in his native garb", who called regularly selling his Madras curry. He must have been an exotic figure wandering through the narrow Island lanes.

MACARONI CHEESE

Half a pound of tomatoes, one tablespoon curry powder, a quarter of a pound of macaroni, two ounces butter, salt and pepper, two ounces grated cheese. Put the macaroni into salted boiling water, boil it thirty minutes, and drain it. Scald the tomatoes, peel and slice them. Put the butter in a saucepan to melt, add sliced tomatoes and macaroni, stir well together, add pinch of salt and curry powder. Lastly, with two forks stir in the grated cheese for five minutes, then serve.

~~~~~~~

SAVOURY RICE WITH CHEESE

Wash *three ounces of rice* and boil it in milk until tender, adding pepper and salt. Butter a pie-dish, spread half the rice on it, sprinkle *an ounce of grated cheese* on it, add the rest of the rice and another ounce of cheese, put *little pieces of butter* on the top, and brown in a medium oven, 300F, Mark 2—3.

~~~~~~~

CHEESE STRAWS

Two ounces of butter, two ounces of flour, one yolk of an egg, three ounces of cheese (two ounces of Parmesan and one ounce of Cheddar), one tablespoon of cold water, cayenne pepper, salt. Rub the butter into the flour, add the grated cheese, pepper and salt, mix to the consistency of pastry with the yolk and water; roll out, and cut into rings and straws, allowing six straws to one ring. Bake about 10 minutes in a medium to hot oven, 370—400F, Mark 5—6, and serve with the straws through the rings. They can brown quickly so keep an eye on them.

~~~~~~~

ROYAL RECIPES

To make a Cake the way of
The Royal Princess, The Lady Elizabeth,
Daughter to King Charles the First

Princess Beatrice Cakes

Prince Consort Pudding

The Royal House has always kept a watchful eye on the Island, aware of its importance in the defence of the south coast of the mainland. Carisbrooke Castle was the fortress and home of the royal representatives, first the Lords, then, from the seventeenth century, the Governors, who have served to the present day. Two of the following recipes are associated with the Castle. I lived for over twenty years in the fourteenth century tower that completes the medieval domestic buildings remaining today. Our living room was Princess Beatrice's library when she was governor of the Island. The room beneath was her dining room and in earlier times it had been King Charles I's bedroom from where he had made his first attempt to escape from imprisonment.

The first recipe is a yeast cake dedicated to Princess Elizabeth, daughter of King Charles, who, after the execution of her father, lived in the castle for only one month during August 1650. Never healthy, she caught a chill and, on the morning of the 8th of September, she was found lying dead in her small bedroom, her head resting on her open Bible. Elizabeth was buried in Newport parish church. Her plain wooden coffin was found when the present Victorian church was built. Today a rather beautiful monument, given by Queen Victoria, marks her tomb. It shows the sleeping princess lying with her head on her Bible and has a touching charm that seems to reflect the character of this sad royal child.

It is impossible to believe that Princess Elizabeth ever made this cake attributed to her, but it is a reminder of the happier days of her childhood. I give the original recipe, then a modern version.

TO MAKE A CAKE THE WAY OF THE
ROYAL PRINCESS, THE LADY ELIZABETH,
DAUGHTER TO KING CHARLES THE FIRST

Take half a peck of Flower (a peck was the equivalent of two gallons, 20 lb. in weight), half a pint of Rose-water, a pint of Ale-yeast, a pint of Cream, boil it, a pound and a half of Butter, six eggs (leave out the whites), four pounds of Currans, one half pound of Sugar, one Nutmeg, and a little Salt, work it very well, and let it stand half an hour by the fire, and then work it up again, and then make it up, and let it stand an hour and a half in the Oven; let not your Oven be too hot.

From *The Queen's Closet Opened* published 1662

MODERN VERSION

½ lb. plain flour, ¼ gill rose-water,* ½ oz. yeast, ½ gill milk, 1½ ozs. butter, 1 egg, 4 ozs. currants, 2 ozs. sugar, ¼ nutmeg, grated, salt. Warm the milk until it is just hot to your finger, add 1 teaspoon sugar and the yeast, and stir well. Leave it in a warm place until there is a froth over the top. Have ready a warm mixing bowl. Sift into it the flour, nutmeg, sugar and salt, and rub in the butter. Stir in the yeast mixture, the beaten egg, and the rose-water. Knead well until it is smooth. Put the dough into a greased bowl, cover with a damp cloth and leave to rise in a warm place until it has doubled in size (about one hour). Now beat down the dough to remove the air and knead in the currants thoroughly. Put into a greased 2-lb. loaf or cake tin. Cover with a cloth and set in a warm place to prove for about 30 minutes. The dough should spring back when lightly pressed with a floured finger. Cook in a pre-heated oven at 400F, Mark 6, for 35 minutes. Although this is called a cake, it is really a light bun-loaf. Cut into slices and butter.

* You can buy rose-water from health food shops or chemists.

~~~~~~~

Just over two hundred and fifty years later a second Princess came to live in Carisbrooke Castle. She was Princess Beatrice, then governor of the Isle of Wight, an office she accepted following the death of her husband, Prince Henry of Battenburg, in 1896. Her dining room, now the lecture room, remains in structure very much as she would remember it. A large mullioned window looks onto the courtyard, filling the room with light, and opposite is a minstrels' gallery. Double doors beneath the gallery open into a narrow passage from which the back stairs lead down to a vast kitchen in which stands a mammoth 'Kitchener', now black and silent, but once hissing and crackling as it heated, boiled and roasted for the household.

Princess Beatrice would certainly have taken an interest in the work that went on there. Cooking was part of her education at Osborne House, where the pretty kitchen of the Swiss Cottage had been the perfect place to learn. She liked cooking and was good at it, so that when a cake was dedicated to her in the 1880s we can safely assume that this princess was quite capable of baking it herself.

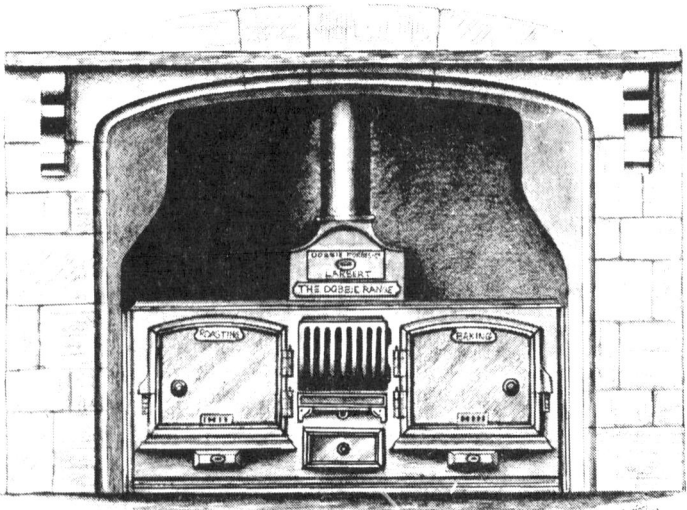

The Kitchener in Carisbrooke Castle by Frank Basford.

PRINCESS BEATRICE CAKES

Take 1½ lbs. of butter, 2 lbs. of castor sugar, the yolk of 20 eggs and the white of 10 eggs, 1¾ lbs. of flour and the grated rinds of 4 oranges; cream the butter and sugar together, add the yolks and the grated rinds of the oranges, have the whites of the eggs well beaten. Then add the flour and stir all gently together; put into hoops nicely papered, and bake in a moderate oven; ice them over when cold, and pipe with icing coloured with a little carmine.

From *The Pastrycook and Confectioner's Guide*
quoted in *The Shy Princess* by David Duff

MODERN VERSION

6 ozs. butter, 8 ozs. castor sugar, 5 egg yolks, 2 egg whites, 7 ozs. self-raising flour, grated rind of one orange. Beat the butter and sugar, add the egg yolks and the orange rind. Beat the egg whites and fold in. Add the flour gently. Put into small, greased paper cases and bake in a moderate oven for 15−20 minutes. Ice when cold. The cakes are light, golden in colour, deliciously orangey, and very Victorian with their pink and white icing. Perfect for a children's tea party.

~~~~~~~

My last Royal Recipe is named after Princess Beatrice's father, Prince Albert. When Queen Victoria decided that Osborne should be their island home, he dedicated his time to designing and directing the rebuilding of the house and the laying out of the estate. He made the home farm a model for the local landowners. At the end of a busy day in the open Albert would cheerfully sit down and "eat loads of dinner". He would certainly have enjoyed this pudding, named after him. A good steamed sponge, it emerges from the cooking a golden mound, speckled with currants and glazed with a rich marmalade sauce.

75

PRINCE CONSORT PUDDING
1845

Take *three eggs, the same weight of butter, flour, sugar.*
Beat the butter to a cream, adding the sugar and egg
yolks. Beat the whites to a firm froth, adding them
gently to the mixture. Then add the flour, the same
weight of *currants, mixed peel,* flavour with *a few drops
of vanilla essence.* Butter a mould and spread it quickly
with *marmalade.* Steam for three hours. I reduce the
quantity by a third, using one large egg as the standard
weight and steam this size pudding for 1¾ hours. This
will feed four small appetites or three hearty ones.

Osborne House

76

"RECEIPTS" FROM NUNWELL

To bake Herrings
To stew Eels

To boil a Capon and Marrow Bones
To make a Rabitt-Pye

To make a White Sellibub
To make Lemmon Creame
An other Biskett where of King James
and his Queene have often eate

To make a Paste of Viollets or Gillyflowers
Marmalett of Orrangs
Marmalade of Cherries
To make Gooseberry Wine

Nunwell House, near Brading, is the home of the Oglander family, who settled on the Island in Norman times. These recipes are taken, by the kind permission of Mrs. Oglander, from one of their treasures, a beautiful handwritten 'receipt' book compiled by one of the Oglander ladies (with some additions from other interested people) in the eighteenth century. I retain the original wording and spelling, giving modern versions of some of the recipes when necessary, but I believe you will not find them difficult to follow and will be surprised how different and delicious they taste.

The book is large, ten and a half inches in length and eight and a half in breadth. It is bound in black leather, elegantly decorated with simple gold line tooling and closed with silver clasps. One section of the spine is in Turkey red leather and has the word RECEIPTS printed on it in gold. These letters have been laid on in a very irregular and unskilled way; added to which the entire binding has been put on back to front, so that in order to read the contents you have to turn the book over! So it seems likely that the binding was the work of an amateur. Inside, the pages are divided into cookery recipes and medicinal cures. Each page of recipes is set elegantly within a frame of carefully drawn margins.

Some of the recipes date from the seventeenth century and these would have been enjoyed by the most famous member of the family, Sir John Oglander, who kept a diary and remained loyal to his King throughout the stormy times of the Civil War. Sir John was a respected local gentleman and he kept up the style of living that was expected of him, but in his household there was no room for extravagance. He includes three recipes in his notebooks: calves' feet in batter, fried whiting, and roast mutton — the food of a plain man, quite unlike the elaborate dishes that would be prepared for special occasions.

He had the support of a perfect wife, Frances. She did not, Sir John writes, belong to the "Fare high and well and do nothing" class of woman; she was the true lady: "I could never have done it (lived within his income) without a careful wife who was no spender, never wore a silk gown but for credit when she went abroad, and never to please herself. She was up every day before me and oversaw all the out-houses; she would not trust her maid with directions but wet her shoes to see it done herself. Yet I always kept a good house, not much inferior to any in this island." Lady Oglander was the model of what was expected from the women who lived in manor houses throughout the kingdom; who managed their families and servants well, supervised the gardens, the dairies, the still-room and the kitchens, and kept large and busy households contented and happy.

Lady Frances Oglander, wife of Sir John Oglander of Nunwell, 1585–1655. Photograph by kind permission of the Oglander family.

TO BAKE HERRINGS

(Clean and prepare the fish.) Season them well *with Pepper and Salt* and cover them *with an Equal Quantity of Port Wine and Vinegar* and bake them the Same Time as Household Bread (in a hot oven, 425—450F, Mark 7, for 10—15 minutes). You may add two or three Bay Leaves.

Mrs. Fox

~~~~~~~

TO STEW ELLES

When your Eles are striped, gutt them and cut them in pieces (your fishmonger may prepare the Eels for you) and put them in a Skillet (large saucepan) with *as much water and Salt as will cover them,* set them on the fire (burner) and let them boyle a little, then poure away allmost all the liquor from them, and put (add) to them *as much white wine as will cover them and a bundle of sweet herbs* (see p. 16), *and some Parsley, and a little Onion, and some Cloves,* stew them alltogether till they bee tender — about 45 minutes. (A skillet was a metal saucepan with three or four legs and a long handle which could be used for cooking in an open fireplace. I remember seeing them as a child in Wales.)

TO BOYLE A CAPON AND MARROW-BONES

Take a Capon and Marrow-bones, and whatsoever you will, Liver, Gizzards and Pinions, and boyle them all together in a Pott, and against they are boyled ready, have readie the Sauce, which must be a pound of sweete butter at least, stirred with a little Vinagare and Sugar to your liking, then take the yolks of tenn Eggs boyled hard and minced verry small, and a little Parsley boyled and minced small, and some Lemmon-pill minced, and some Mustard, and when it is ready put it upon the Meate.

MODERN VERSION
Serves four people

Take *a 3-lb. chicken, or boiling fowl, and two or three large marrow bones.* If you have a large enough pan, put them in together with *salt and a few peppercorns* and boil gently for about two hours. (I boil the marrow bones separately and then put the chicken, plus the gizzard, heart and liver, into a slow cooker with the bone stock and leave it to cook overnight.) Take out the chicken after it has boiled, and keep warm.

SAUCE

Melt *two ounces of butter* in a pan. Add *1 tablespoon of vinegar and sugar to taste. Boil one or two heads of parsley* for 1—2 minutes and then chop very finely. Break up *two hard-boiled eggs* with a fork. Add to them the chopped parsley and *finely grated rind of a lemon.* Put this mixture, with *a taste of mustard added,* into the melted butter and stir together. You can pour this sauce over the chicken or hand it round in a sauce boat. It adds a piquant sweet-sour flavour to the chicken. This dish is also very good eaten cold. The broth in which the chicken is cooked makes the basis of an excellent soup, so you will find this a delicious and economical recipe.

Together with castles and the Domesday Book, the Norman conquerors have left us the rabbit. They brought the useful little beast over to England to provide fur and food for the upper classes. The earliest record in the Island of rabbits, or coneys as the adults were known, occurs in 1225 and refers to a coney keeper on the manor of Bowcombe, about a mile from Carisbrooke Castle. His job was to protect the warren and manage the rabbits, presumably trying to persuade them not to stray too far from home. But of course they did stray and soon the rabbit population on the Island was enormous as there were no foxes to keep them down until they too were imported, this time for hunting, in the nineteenth century.

In Elizabethan days, the Island rabbits were killed and taken to London by the coney man who came regularly for fresh supplies. He also acted as postman, taking letters up to the capital and bringing the London mail back with him — a kind of 'coney-express'! This recipe, for a rich rabbit pie eaten at Nunwell, reminds us that for many centuries rabbit was the food of the gentry.

The Coney Man by Frank Basford.

TO MAKE A RABBIT-PYE

Take two rabbitts clean washed, cut them in pieces about a fingars length, then take Salt and strew on them, take Parsley, sweete Marierome Pennyroall of each half a dozen spriggs, mince them verry small and put them upon your meate, and fill your pye putting in butter, soe bake it, when it is baked have readie, as you cutt it up, a pint of white wine and three Eggs well beaten and a good spoonfull of Sugar. Stirr all these well together, and put it into your Pye. Then set it into the Oven for a quarter of an hour. (It is difficult to know when the pastry lid was put on. They cannot mean that the pie was completely sliced up after the first cooking! Possibly they mean that the wine sauce was put in through gashes made in the pastry.)

MODERN VERSION

Take *two young rabbits (jointed) or 1 lb. of boned rabbit.* Put the rabbit meat to soak in cold water, covering it completely. If possible change the water once or twice; leave to soak overnight. Rinse the meat and pack the pieces into a deep pie dish but leave plenty of room for the sauce to be added. Add herbs to your liking (I use a mixture of dried parsley, thyme, marigold and bay, tied in a bag and set in the middle of the meat — they give the pie a delicious flavour). Add *about 4–6 ozs. butter or margarine and a little water.* Cover with foil and cook in a moderate oven for 1½–2 hours. Take it out at the end of cooking and allow to cool. Make your wine sauce with *a pint of white wine, three well-beaten eggs and sugar to taste* and add to the pie. Cover with pastry and return to the oven for fifteen minutes or until the pastry is cooked.

~~~~~~~

TO MAKE A WHITE SELLIBUB

Take to *a pint of cream a quarter of a pint of Sack, or White wine, the juice of half a Lemmon, the white of an egg beaten to froth, with as much suger as will sweeten it* mingle these together, and beat it up to a froth, with a whisk verry clean made with Birch, or a sprigg of Rosemary (or a fork), and as the froth rises take it of with a spoone and put it into a Sellibub pott (wine glasses) and soe doe untill it be all done, it must stand two houres before you spend it (eat it).

~~~~~~~

TO MAKE LEMMON CREAME

Take half a pound of double refined Suger, the juice of two Lemmons, seaven spoonfulls of Conduit-water — set it over he fire till it is dissolved, then strain it through Flannell. then put the white of three Eggs into it. then set over the fire again, til it thicken but not boyle.

Mrs. Eliza Leigh

MODERN VERSION

This is a simple quick recipe. Take *¼ lb. sugar, juice of one lemon, 3 tablespoons of water.* Heat the ingredients gently until the sugar has melted. Separate *the white of one large egg and part of another* and add to the syrup. Beat in the whites using a twig whisk or a fork. The mixture froths up into bubbles. Heat it gently for about 10 minutes until it thickens. If the mixture boils, some of the egg white will separate into solid globules, but you can overcome this by removing the pan from the heat and beating the mixture well with a rotary whisk. The final consistency is like single cream.

~~~~~~~

AN OTHER BISKETT WHERE OF KING JAMES
AND HIS QUEENE HAVE OFTEN EATE
WITH MUCH LIKING

Take a pound and a quarter of Sugar, and a pound of Flower verry finely boulted and after verry finely serced. you must beat the Sugar verry fine and then you must serce it through a Lawne Sercer, then mingle the flower and the Sugar together. And then take twelve Eggs, whereof you must take the white of half, that is 6 whites. First beat the Eggs with three or Foure spoon-fulls of Rosewater. Then put your flower and your Sugar that are mingled together, to your Eggs, and then beat them two houres together. And a little before you put them in the Oven, put a few Carraway seeds and Anniseeds into it. And butter the Plates before you put on the Stuff. And your Oven must bee noe hotter than is heat for a Tart.

Lady Parsons

MODERN VERSION

5 ozs. sugar, 4 ozs. plain flour, 1 whole egg and 1 egg white, 2 teaspoons rose-water. Mix the sugar and the flour together. Beat the eggs with the rose-water. Add to the flour and sugar and beat very well for about 10—15 minutes. The mixture is very soft. Drop a teaspoonful for each biscuit on to a well-greased tray, allowing room for the biscuits to spread. Bake in a moderate oven, 340F, Mark 4, for 10—15 minutes. They should be pale gold in the centre and deeper gold at the edges. As I don't have a small boy in my kitchen to sit beating my mixture for two hours, I have to rely on my electric beater or rotary hand beater — they cope equally well! These are very good thin biscuits that go well with ices or creamy puddings.

~~~~~~~~

STILL-ROOM RECIPES

It was in the still-room that a very special part of housekeeping went on. As the name suggests, the main work was distillation, capturing the essences of flowers and herbs in tiny drops of liquid that trickled through the glass stills. In this quiet room, separated from the rest of the busy household, the housewife prepared toilet waters, scented soaps, wines, as well as jams, jellies, pickles, preserves, and the family medicines.

Fruits, flowers and herbs were the material of the still-room. The English were noted for their love of flowers, both outside and in the house. In Summer the flowers came creeping in through doors and windows, sometimes as a live decoration trained to climb round the inside of a bay window, or standing in green banks before the empty fireplace and decorating window ledges in little pots and jugs. But in the still-room they were put to practical use, and when they were in perfect bloom, garden and field flowers were gathered, violets, primroses, cowslips, elderflowers, marigolds. But most of all the rose. As these recipes show, rose-water was widely used in cooking and it was also used for cosmetic purposes.

Standing before her long tables, surrounded by stills, great glass jars, large mixing bowls, pestle and mortars, the housewife turned the sweet-smelling flowers and herbs of Summer into luxuries to delight her family throughout the long Winter months.

Few of us have time to distil these days, but here is a recipe for making delightful flower decorations. You might like to try it to decorate a cake for a really special occasion.

TO MAKE A PASTE OF VIOLLETS,
OR GILLIFLOWERS, OR ANY OTHER FLOWERS

Take blew garden violetts, pick them (remove any with blemishes), stamp them (crush them well — a pestle and mortar was used), then take six ounces of Double refined Sugar (very fine sugar) with as much Rose-water as will wet it, then boyle it to a Candie-height (to the heat for Candy), then put in the Flowers being finely beaten, so lett it boyle, stirring it till it bee thick; then power (pour) it upon a wett plate; and when it is cold, stamp all the crumbs to a fine powder, and serce (sift) it, and make it into paste with Gum-dragon (gum tragacanth) steeped in Rose-water; then roule it thinn and print it (cut it into the shapes you want), and dry it.

Mrs. Joyce

The true gillyflowers were the old-fashioned clove-scented cottage pinks. Later, wallflowers and white stock were also called 'gillys'.

~~~~~~~

MARMALETT OF ORRANG'S

(This is really an apple and orange jelly. I have interpreted the 'water of Pippins' as apple juice.) Take *two pounds of Sugar, a pint of Running water, a Pint of the water of Pippins, one pound and a half of Pippins coard and Quartered,* put them together, boyle them till the Pippins bee tender, then put in *half a pound of sliced Orranges,* and boyle them alltogether till they bee nere enough (nearly cooked); then put in *eight or ten spoonefulls of Orrange or Leamon Juice,* boyle it to a tender Jelly and take it up. Muske and Ambergriece doe well in it.

~~~~~~~

87

MARMALADE OF CHERRIES

Take your Cherries and stone them, cut them in pieces, weigh them, and to *every two pound of Cherries, take a pound of Suger,* and put them in a clean skillet (sauce-pan), and let it boyle softly, stirring it often, and soe boyle it to Marmalade, then take it up and put it in Glasses, and let it stand in a warm place, the space of a weeke, then cover it up.

~~~~~~~~

TO MAKE GOOSEBERRY WINE

Take *to every quart of water, three pound of Goose-berrys, and a pound of Suger,* bruise the Gooseberries, and steepe them (in water) twentie foure houres stirring it often, then let the liquor run through a hair Seive, into an Earthen pann, and put the Suger to it, let it bee verry close covered for a fortnight or 3 weekes, then draw it into bottles and close corke it, and tye it downe, in three months or less it will bee readie to drink.

~~~~~~~~

FROM A FISHERMAN'S HUT

Mackerel in Brine
Fried Cockles
Prawns
Bass in Cider
Oyster or Mussel Loaf

In the seas around the Island enormous catches of fish were made throughout the nineteenth century, but probably because the Islanders were used to cooking very fresh fish (few had facilities to store it), they were able to cook it simply and there are very few recipes for more elaborate dishes. But they cooked their fish well, as I discovered when I asked a fisherman friend, Clifford Matthews. He combines the past and the present in his own life. As well as sailing and fishing, he is a fine woodworker. He reconstructed the wooden carriage on which The Carisbrooke Falcon — the eighteenth century parish gun — now rests in Carisbrooke Castle Museum, as well as working on the replica of *The Golden Hind.* When he told me the following recipes he added the pungent comment, "The trouble with women cooks is that they will go fidgeting and fussing with things — adding this and that. All fish needs is plain cooking to bring out the flavour". Perhaps some men cooks might share the same failing when let loose in the kitchen! But of course he is right to say that when fish is really fresh, simple cooking is best — but this has to be carefully done.

MACKEREL IN BRINE

Mackerel is a rich, oily fish. Cooked in this way, the oil is drawn out into the water and the flavour of the fish can be enjoyed to the full. Fishermen and sailors need only catch their mackerel and put it into a pot of fresh sea water. Those of us on land must buy the freshest mackerel we can and make our own brine, judging for ourselves the necessary saltiness. I add one tablespoon of salt to one pint of water. Boil the mackerel in this water for ten minutes. Drain and eat immediately.

~~~~~~~

FRIED COCKLES

The secret of producing cockles that are really good to eat, Clifford Matthews tells me, is to wash, wash, wash, and then when you have done that to wash them again, so that you get rid of all the sand! When you have done this, leave them in salted water overnight. Wash them again four or five times. Boil the cockles for 10 minutes. Roll them in breadcrumbs and fry with bacon.

~~~~~~~~

PRAWNS

Put your prawns into boiling water and cook for 3 minutes. Turn them into a colander to drain and then dredge them with salt. Shake them thoroughly — as you would a lettuce — to remove the excess water completely. This leaves the prawns really crisp and you can adjust the salt to taste.

~~~~~~~~

If you find a silvery bass in the fishmonger's it is well worth buying. They can weigh from 2—3 lbs. and their flesh is firm. The smaller bass can be grilled or fried but this recipe is for a large whole fish, which is best cooked in the oven.

BASS IN CIDER

Take off the head. Grease a casserole thoroughly with butter. Lay the fish in it, *add a bay leaf, a few pickling spice and enough cider to cover the fish generously.* Cover securely with cooking foil and cook gently, 325F, Mark 3, for about 30 minutes. You can treat bass steaks in the same way, in which case, reduce the cooking time to 15 minutes.

Oysters have been eaten by the Islanders since Roman times and by the sixteenth century they were so plentiful that they were part of everyday life. The 'oyster draggers' who worked the River Medina down to the mouth at Cowes were licensed to sell their catch at 2d (1p) a hundred oysters in Queen Elizabeth I's reign. As the usual rate of pay for the ordinary workman was 3s (15p) a week, the oysters came at a bargain price!

In the eighteenth century when it was election day in the old borough of Newtown, the burgesses sat down at noon in the Town Hall to enjoy an oyster luncheon. This was provided from the oyster beds at Newtown harbour by the elector who was then working the beds. After a short interval a substantial cold dinner was served and then came the election. The chairman produced from his pocket a card naming the two new members of parliament. They were at once proposed and seconded and "their health was drunk with the utmost enthusiasm". And so the election was made!

You can still see the Town Hall today in Newtown, a charming brick building, and inside you will find the room where the electors sat to eat their oyster lunch. The oyster fisheries are still in the haven too, continuing a tradition that reaches back to the Middle Ages.

OYSTER OR MUSSEL LOAF

Take *one bloomer loaf (a long white loaf with a floury crust)* and cut it lengthways across the two ends and along one long side so that you can raise the upper part like a lid. Take out the soft middle of the loaf and *brush the inside with melted butter. Cut up ½ lb. streaky bacon into pieces about one inch in size* and fry. *Cut ½ lb. of tomatoes* into similar sizes and fry. *Fry twelve oysters.* Put all the ingredients into the loaf and add the gravy from the cooking pan. Close the bread lid and wrap the loaf firmly in foil. Bake in a medium oven for 30–40 minutes. The same recipe may be used for mussels.

~~~~~~~

FAVOURITES FROM
ISLE OF WIGHT COUNTY, U.S.A.

Southern Fried Chicken
Chicken Soup
Pork Chops and Apple Rings
Green Beans and Bacon Bites
Spoon Bread
Grandma's Fried Cymblins
Peach Cobbler

I was delighted when I discovered that an American friend, Virginia Abbott, newly-arrived in our Isle of Wight, had been brought up in Isle of Wight County, U.S.A. She spent a happy time researching among the recipes her mother had cooked when she was a girl, growing up in Smithfield, the main town. From these I have chosen some that she tells me were everyone's favourites.

In some of these recipes you will see similarities with our English recipes because, as you might expect, some of the first settlers in that part of Virginia (my friend's name is highly appropriate!) were sent by a company organized by two gentlemen from the Isle of Wight. They were Sir Richard Worsley, who lived at Appledurcombe, and Robert Newland, a prosperous merchant from Newport. They dispatched Captain Christopher Lawne with a party of emigrants in 1618 with instructions to set up a 'plantation'. Although the spot he chose was low-lying and swampy, somehow the little community survived. Known at first as 'Lawne's Plantation', it was renamed Isle of Wight Plantation in 1620, and later Isle of Wight County.

Isle of Wight County became famous for its pigs and Queen Victoria had a regular order of Smithfield hams brought across the Atlantic for the royal table. So pork and bacon recipes are included, but I must begin with the most popular of all American recipes — Southern Fried Chicken.

SOUTHERN FRIED CHICKEN

Meaty pieces from a 2½—3 lb. chicken, ½ cup flour, 1 cup milk, ¾ teaspoon salt, pepper to taste, melted lard to cover the bottom of an iron skillet (solid-bottomed saucepan) to a depth of ¼ inch. Wash the chicken pieces and pat dry with paper towels. Place them in a shallow bowl with the milk and turn them over to coat them with the milk. Place flour, salt and pepper in a small paper or plastic bag. Place the chicken pieces in the bag and shake it about so that the chicken is well coated with the savoury flour. Have ready the skillet with the hot lard in it. Brown the chicken pieces on both sides, then reduce the heat and cover the skillet. Cook for about fifteen to twenty minutes. Remove the cover to crisp the chicken, turning the pieces for an extra minute or two. Remove to a platter and keep warm.

GRAVY

Pour off all the fat from the skillet, except for one tablespoon, taking care not to lose any of the little bits of 'goodies' from the chicken meat left in the skillet. Turn up the heat slightly and add *1 tablespoon of flour, salt and pepper.* Stir the mix, scraping the bottom of the skillet. Allow to brown slightly, add *the remaining milk* from coating the chicken pieces and stir until the gravy thickens.

~~~~~~~~

CHICKEN SOUP

Make this soup when you prepare your Southern Fried Chicken, as it uses all the pieces you do not need for that recipe. *Back, neck and wings of a 2½—3 lb. chicken (I use the whole carcase of the chicken when the joints have been removed), 1 large onion, sliced, 1 stalk of celery, leaves and stem, chopped, ¾ cup uncooked rice or 1 cup noodles, water to cover, salt and pepper to taste.*

Place water, chicken, onion and celery in a large pot. Bring to boiling point, lower the heat and cook until the meat falls easily from the bones. Take off the heat and leave to cool. Remove the meat from the bones and while the meat and bones are out of the soup, skim off the fat from the liquid. Return the meat to the pot and bring it to the boil again. Add the rice or noddles, salt and pepper, and cook until the rice is done, or the noodles tender but not mushy. Add more water for a thinner soup.

~~~~~~~

PORK CHOPS AND APPLE RINGS

4 pork chops, a little flour for dredging, 1 tablespoon shortening (lard), salt and pepper. Trim half the fat from the chops and place this in a skillet (strong-bottomed saucepan or frying pan) together with the lard. Cook the trimmings gently until the fat runs freely. Remove the unwanted rinds. Wipe the chops with damp paper towels and dredge them in flour, shaking off any excess. Brown the chops both sides. Reduce the heat and cook until done. Season with salt and pepper and remove to a platter and keep warm.

APPLE RINGS

4 or more medium-sized cooking apples, a little brown sugar, flour and cinnamon. While the chops are cooking, wash and dry the apples. Core, but do not pare (peel) them. Slice crosswise into 1-cm (just under ½-inch) slices. Dredge these in flour, using up any left over from dredging the chops. Fry, a few at a time, over a medium heat in the fat left in the skillet, adding more lard if necessary. Cook until they are brown on both sides. Remove to the platter with the chops. Sprinkle the apple rings with brown sugar and cinnamon to taste.

~~~~~~~

Beans and maize were part of the native Indians' food and they showed the early settlers how to grow both crops together. First, they planted the maize seeds in clusters of four in straight rows, then when the maize was about a foot high, they planted the beans between them so they could grow up the corn stalks.

GREEN BEANS AND BACON BITES

Choose young beans. Wash them and break off the stem end. Break each bean into bite-size pieces. Cook in a small amount of salted water in a covered saucepan. Meanwhile, cut *two or three rashers of streaky bacon* into small pieces and fry until crisp. When the beans are done, but still crisp, drain off the water. Add the bacon pieces and drippings to the beans and allow to stand covered for a few minutes. Turn into a bowl and serve warm.

~~~~~~~

SPOON BREAD

Note: 1 breakfast cup of flour, lightly filled, equals ¼ lb; 1 breakfast cup of liquid equals ½ pint. *1½ cups cornmeal,* 1 cup water, 2 cups milk, 1½ teaspoons salt, 5 eggs, 2 tablespoons melted butter, 2 tablespoons baking powder, 1½ teaspoons sugar.* Grease a large shallow baking dish. Combine the water and milk and bring to simmering point. Add the cornmeal, salt, sugar and butter, and stir over a medium heat until the mixture thickens (about five minutes). Remove from the heat. Beat the eggs in a bowl with the baking powder until very light and fluffy. Add to the cornmeal mixture and stir in. Pour into the prepared dish and bake for 45–50 minutes at 350F, Mark 4. Serve hot with lots of butter. It is particularly good with pork or seafood.

* Sold in most health food shops.

~~~~~~~

Cymblins are little squashes, sometimes called 'patty-pans' (they look just like them) in Isle of Wight County. They are not everyday items in our greengrocers as they are there, but you will be able to find them in the larger stockists.

GRANDMA'S FRIED CYMBLINS

4 medium cymblins, 1 medium-size onion, salt and pepper, 2 tablespoons shortening (lard). Wash and cut the cymblins into small pieces, cutting away the stem end. Place in a saucepan with enough water to cover them and cook until tender but not mushy. Meanwhile, peel the onion and mince it. Cook in the lard until translucent. When the cymblins are cooked drain them and mash them thoroughly. Add to the onion and brown over a medium heat, stirring to prevent the vegetables sticking. Serve warm.

~~~~~~~

PEACH COBBLER
Serves six—eight people

½ cup melted butter, 1 cup self-raising flour, 1 cup sugar, 1 cup milk, a little grated nutmeg, ½ teaspoon vanilla essence, 1 quart fresh peaches, peeled, stoned and sliced. First cook the peaches very slightly in a little water and put to one side. Pour the butter into a 3—4 pint baking dish. Mix the flour, sugar, milk, nutmeg and vanilla, and pour it over the butter. Add the peaches, drained and sweetened to taste. Bake for 45 minutes at 350F, Mark 4, until golden brown and bubbly.

~~~~~~~

THE TRADITION TODAY

Salmon Puff
Potted Cheese Spread
Bacon Savoury
Daddy's Omelette
Owl Cottage Cherry Meringue
Sugared Custard Biscuits

Hanover Biscuits
Lindy Cakes
Wight Ice
Honey Cakes
Melting Fingers
Honey Truffles

Today original and imaginative cooks are adding interesting new recipes to this rich tradition of Island cookery.
I asked some of my Island friends for their favourites
and here is a selection of modern recipes we have
enjoyed together.

SALMON PUFF

*One 7½-oz. tin of red salmon, 1 lb. puff pastry, 1 egg
(separated into white and yolk), 1 teaspoon chopped
parsley, 1 oz. white breadcrumbs, 3 teaspoons lemon
juice, salt and black pepper, 1 clove.* Strain juice from
the salmon and remove the skin and bones. Mash the
salmon with a fork and add the lightly beaten egg yolk,
breadcrumbs, lemon juice, parsley and seasoning. Mix
well. Roll out the puff pastry thinly. Cut just under
half into the shape of a fish. With the remaining pastry
cut a rather larger shape — this will be the top. Place
the salmon mixture on the smaller shape, keeping it
within ½ an inch of the edge. Brush the edges with egg
white and cover with the top shape, making sure the
edges are well sealed. Put in the clove for the eye.
Brush over with egg or milk and bake in a pre-heated
oven, 400F, Mark 5, until golden brown — about
½ an hour. This dish is equally good hot or cold. If
you are serving it hot it is delicious with a Bechamel
sauce, substituting the salmon juice for some of the milk.

BECHAMEL SAUCE

This is a basic white sauce made with flavoured milk.
First you prepare the milk. Pour *1 pint of milk* into a
saucepan. Add to it *half a small onion, sliced, 6 peppercorns, a small bay leaf, and a blade of mace. You can
also add a small piece of carrot and a small piece of
celery.* Bring the milk slowly to the boil. Remove the
saucepan from the heat, cover it, and leave the ingredients to infuse the milk with their flavour for about 15
minutes. Strain the milk into a jug and it is ready for

use. To make the sauce: take *1½ ozs. butter, 1 oz. plain flour, 1 pint prepared milk, salt and pepper.* Heat the butter gently − it must melt but not brown. Take it off the heat and stir in the flour. Beat the mixture well until smooth. Return the saucepan to the heat and add the milk gradually, beating it thoroughly into the flour so that the mixture is smooth. (If lumps do form they can be removed by beating well with a rotary whisk or electric blender.) When the mixture has absorbed all the milk cook the sauce gently for five minutes and add seasoning to taste.

Joyce Bale, Carisbrooke

~~~~~~~~

POTTED CHEESE SPREAD

4 ozs. butter, 8 ozs. grated Cheddar cheese, ½ teaspoon made mustard, a few drops of Worcester Sauce, milk, salt and pepper. Cream the butter well, then add salt, pepper, mustard, cheese and Worcester Sauce. Beat in sufficient milk to make a smooth paste. Chill. This mixture can also be shaped into a sausage, covered in chopped almonds or walnuts and cut into slices. To vary the taste try adding chopped chives.

Joyce Bale, Carisbrooke

BACON SAVOURY
Serves two people

8 rashers of streaky bacon, 2 ozs. fine fresh breadcrumbs, 1 teaspoon parsley, 1 teaspoon thyme, salt and pepper, grated rind of half a lemon, 1 egg. Blend the dry ingredients with the beaten egg and add a little milk if the mixture seems too dry. Leave this for about half an hour to swell. Cut off the rind from the bacon. Grease a square tin and lay four rashers in it. Divide the filling into four and spread it evenly on the bacon. Cover with the remaining bacon. Cook for about 30 minutes in the oven at 325F, Mark 3. Dried herbs can be used successfully.

Una Samuel

~~~~~~~

DADDY'S OMELETTE

This was cooked by my fisherman friend, Clifford Matthews, when he was left at home to cook for his sons. Break *one egg* and beat it well. Take *one slice of bread* and rub it into crumbs. Mix it with the egg and stir well until the mixture is soft. Add *salt and pepper* to taste. Lightly grease a frying pan and heat it. Pour in the mixture, press it down firmly and cook like a pancake until it is golden brown. This is sufficient for one person and very good eaten with bacon.

Clifford Matthews, Niton

~~~~~~~

Sometimes behind a successful recipe lies a story of disaster turned into triumph! Hannah Hutchinson, the creator of my next recipe, was expecting guests for dinner and had made meringues. Alas, as she took them off the tray, the meringues broke into pieces. Undaunted, she set to work and made her first cherry pyramid — the first of many which delight those of us lucky enough to sample this delicious sweet.

OWL COTTAGE CHERRY MERINGUE

10—12 broken meringues, ½—¾ pint beaten cream, ½ lb. butter icing, 1 tin black cherries. Break the meringues into even-sized pieces and build a pyramid of them using alternate layers of cream, cherries, butter icing and meringues. Decorate this pyramid with piped cream and the remaining cherries.

BUTTER ICING

4 ozs. butter (or Krona), 8 ozs. icing sugar. Beat together thoroughly until pale and white.

MERINGUES

3 egg whites, 6 ozs. sugar (3 ozs. granulated, 3 ozs. castor). Beat the whites until they are quite stiff — the mixture should hold its shape on the beater. Beat in the granulated sugar, an ounce at a time, then fold in the castor sugar. Have ready two baking trays, well greased and floured, or line them with non-stick paper. Put spoonfuls of the meringue mixture onto the trays. In this case the shape does not matter. Set the oven at 250—275F, Mark ½—1, and put in the meringues for one hour until they are set. Take out and ease from the tray with a sharp knife, turning them on one side. Return to the oven for about thirty minutes so that the base dries out. Leave on a wire tray to cool.

Hannah Hutchinson, Mottistone

SUGARED CUSTARD BISCUITS

4 ozs. butter or firm margarine, 4 ozs. castor sugar, 1 egg (separated), ¼ teaspoon salt, 6 ozs. plain flour, 1 oz. custard powder, 2 drops vanilla essence, sugar for dredging. Cream the butter and sugar together until light and fluffy, and work in the egg yolk. Add the flour and custard powder. Wrap in greaseproof paper and leave in a cool place to harden. Roll out thinly, stamp out into shapes and place on a greased tray. Beat the egg white slightly. Brush this over the biscuits and dredge with caster sugar. Bake near the top of the oven for 12—15 minutes at 350F, Mark 4. Take out and leave in the baking tray to crisp.

Una Samuel

~~~~~~~~

My next two recipes come from Hanover House, at Brook, a tiny village on the south coast of the Island. Hanover House dates from the seventeenth century and is the ideal place to stop for tea after a walk on the downs or an afternoon on the beach. To sit in the garden, with tea and cakes, overlooking the cluster of houses around the bay, is to savour the special pleasure of a sunny day on the Island. Inside are low-ceilinged rooms with great open hearths where generations have enjoyed good Island cooking and where today you can enjoy new recipes created by Jane Nickerson and her mother.

HANOVER BISCUITS

6 ozs. self-raising flour, ½ teaspoon bicarbonate of soda, ½ teaspoon ground ginger, 3 ozs. castor sugar, 4 ozs. margarine, 1 tablespoon golden syrup. Sieve all the dry ingredients into a bowl. Melt the syrup and margarine in a saucepan, pour into the flour mixture and stir thoroughly. Roll the mixture into small balls, approximately the size of a walnut. Put onto a greased tray and bake for 10—12 minutes at 350F, Mark 4.

LINDY CAKES

5 ozs. self-raising flour, 4 ozs. chopped walnuts, 6 ozs. soft brown sugar, 6 ozs. dates or mixed fruit, 4 ozs. melted margarine, 1 beaten egg. Mix all the dry ingredients together in a bowl. Add the melted margarine and the egg, and stir well. Pour into a greased Swiss Roll tin and cook for 30 minutes at 375F, Mark 5. Allow to cool in the tin and cut into squares.

Jane Nickerson, Hanover House, Brook

WIGHT ICE

1 litre vanilla ice cream, 2 ozs. shelled hazel nuts, 2 ozs. crystallized fruits, finely chopped, or 2 ozs. chopped raisins and glacé cherries, 1 tablespoon brandy or rum or a little vanilla essence, 1 7-oz. carton double cream. Chop the hazel nuts finely (reserving a few for decoration). Put the ice cream into a large basin and pound well until soft enough for the nuts, fruit and brandy (or rum or vanilla essence) to be added and thoroughly mixed into the ice cream. Place this in a container that is suitable for freezing, firming it down well, and freeze until needed. Use a hot knife to ease the ice from its container. Whip up the cream and pipe it over the ice cream. Decorate with the remaining hazel nuts.

Joyce Bale, Carisbrooke

~~~~~~~~

My most lasting impression of the Island which is my home is that it is an island of flowers: crowding to the gates of cottage gardens, massed in great banks of colour beside manor house walls, blowing freely in the sea winds over the downs. And if you visit the Island and would like to capture this special charm to take home, then you must buy some Island honey, full of the flavour and scent of its many flowers. So I end this collection with some honey recipes.

HONEY CAKES

6 ozs. honey, 2 ozs. butter, 8 ozs. plain flour, ½ level teaspoon bicarbonate of soda, grated rind of one lemon, 2 tablespoons of milk (if needed). Heat the honey and butter until they are warm. Pour the mixture into a bowl and let it cool a little. Then sift in the flour, which has been slightly warmed, and the bicarbonate of soda. Add the finely grated lemon rind, and milk if necessary. Mix all the ingredients together and then chill. Turn onto a floured surface and shape into cakes 1½ inches in diameter. Put onto a greased floured tray and bake for 10—15 minutes at 375F, Mark 5. Watch the cooking time carefully because they must not overbake. The cakes should be crisp on the outside and soft inside.

~~~~~~~

MELTING FINGERS

4 ozs. margarine, 2 ozs. honey, 5 ozs. plain flour, coconut and honey for the topping. Beat the honey, margarine and flour in a bowl until light and creamy. Place in a greased Swiss Roll tin and bake for 20—25 minutes at 350F, Mark 4. When cool cut into fingers and spread with coconut and honey.

~~~~~~~

HONEY TRUFFLES

3 ozs. honey, 1½ ozs. butter, 4 ozs. digestive bisuit crumbs, 1 oz. chocolate, almond and rum essence, 1 egg white, chocolate vermicelli. Warm the butter. Mix in the rum and almond essences (a few drops). Stir in the honey and biscuit crumbs. Melt the chocolate over a gentle heat and beat it into the mixture. Form into little sweet shapes and leave them to become firm. Dip them in the beaten egg white and roll in vermicelli. These sweets make delicious and original presents for birthdays and Christmas.

Helena Hewston

~~~~~~~~

INDEX